Does It Make You Want To Buy Something?

Key Concepts in Advertising from a Practitioner's Standpoint.

First Edition

PJ Lehrer

10/12/90

ISBN 978-0-578-06444-4

Acknowledgements

This book is dedicated to the unsung heroes—all the amazing people I was fortunate enough to work with during my years in advertising—colleagues, mentors, and clients, who were so gracious about sharing their knowledge with me. I'm delighted to have the opportunity to pass it along.

It is also dedicated to my students who have helped me to understand what is truly important, and how to articulate it in a way that leads to clarity rather than confusion.

And most importantly, this book is dedicated to my husband, Edward Lindquist, who had faith in me, even when I didn't have faith in myself. I can't imagine mornings without you.

Preface

In 2006, after working for more than 20 years in New York City advertising agencies, I began teaching advertising at New York University.

After reviewing the available textbooks, I realized that while they provided a wealth of fascinating information, they did not connect the dots to show readers how that information becomes actionable in practice. They taught students all about advertising, but not how to create advertising.

This book fills that gap and provides the basic tools that advertising practitioners use to develop strategies for communications plans and creative briefs.

That information is combined with research data that supports it, and both stories and examples to provide further clarification.

It is my hope that this information will inform the next generation of advertising professionals, both client- and agency-side, and guide them in the development of more effective communications.

Good Luck!

Table of Contents

Table of Contents (continued)

Part 1: Target Identification

Chapter 1: Introduction

During my 20+ years working at advertising agencies, I interviewed numerous job candidates, mostly for entry-level positions. One question I always asked during interviews was: "Tell me about an ad you like and why you like it." My goal was to see if candidates could take a point of view and defend it.

One day, in 1998, I was interviewing a young man who had just graduated from college, which would make him about 22 years old. I asked him the question and he replied: "I like the Taco Bell ad with the dog in it." He was referring, of course, to the famous campaign featuring a Chihuahua, which ended with the dog saying the tagline: "Yo quiero Taco Bell!" which translates into "I want Taco Bell!"

Immediately my ears perked up, because I never understood this campaign. What were they trying to say? Dogs like our food? At the same time, I realized the campaign was not intended for me, because I would never eat at Taco Bell. However, this young man was probably a current customer and likely part of the target market the campaign intended to motivate.

So, I got very excited, thinking that I was finally going to be enlightened and asked him: "Really, why?" To which he replied: "It's funny." Hmm, not much help there, so I pressed on. "Do you eat at Taco Bell?" I asked. "Yes," he replied.

Okay, so far, so good. "So, when you see this campaign, does it make you want to eat there more often?" "No," he replied. My response: "It wasn't a very good campaign then, was it?"

Good advertising sells stuff.

This is non-negotiable. The purpose of advertising is to sell things; that's why we create it. This doesn't mean that when you see an ad that you will immediately run out to buy the product or service it advertises. But, if at some point, that ad does not persuade the people it intended to reach to buy something it failed and will be pulled regardless of how many people think it is funny or how many creative awards it wins.

In fact, the Taco Bell Chihuahua campaign was ended abruptly in July 2000 after sales, which were flat in 1999, declined by six percent in the second quarter of 2000.[1] Apparently my job candidate knew more than he realized. This campaign was a failure.

American Express
Another, more recent example of an ad that was entertaining but ineffective comes from American Express. Typically, Amex has superb award-winning campaigns that last decades, courtesy of its long-term agency partner Ogilvy & Mather. The *My Life* campaign, which started in 2005, featured celebrities

in beautifully crafted long-form television commercials (90 seconds) and multi-page magazine inserts. Perhaps the most well-liked of the bunch was the one featuring Ellen DeGeneres working with animals. It was a black and white execution of her going about her day interacting with her co-workers, who were all depicted as various types of animals ranging from kangaroos to turtles.

A two-minute version with interactive components was available on the Amex website, and the spot was voted number seven in TBS's Funniest Commercials of the Year for 2006. Yet, the campaign was pulled in April 2007 amid discussions that "entertainment is not the same thing as engagement."[2]

The campaign that replaced it featured specific benefits geared to a more defined target. My favorite stars Tina Fey trying to get into a first class lounge to meet with Martin Scorsese, when she only has a coach ticket. While she tries to play the celebrity card to no avail, her Amex card does the trick. Since access to airline lounges can get expense for frequent fliers, this benefit is a tangible reward that they are likely to value.

Subway

So, what does work? One campaign that worked for me was the 1998 campaign for Subway sandwich shops that introduced Jared, weight loser extraordinaire. At the time, I had never been in a Subway, which made me a pretty difficult sell. But, as someone who is always looking for practical ways to keep my diet healthy and my weight under control, I took note of the commercial.

One aspect, in particular, resonated—a split-screen shot that showed Jared before and after his weight loss. It was a classic image, of him in profile clearly showing that where he once filled out his pants, nothing but air now existed. It was very impressive; and memorable.

So, I went into a Subway and gave it a try. The sandwich was good, so I became a regular customer. I wasn't the only one. Shortly after the ad began airing, sales jumped by approximately 20 percent.[3]

Perhaps more impressive is that in 2008, Subway trotted Jared out again for a repeat performance in honor of his tenth anniversary. When quizzed about the strategy, Hardy Grewal, owner of the Southern California Subway franchise rights said: "Whenever the sales get sluggish, we say to 'Put Jared back on TV' and the sales go up, every time."[4] Impressive results indeed.

Chapter 2: Selecting Target Markets

The first step in developing an advertising campaign is to thoroughly define your target. Are they male or female? What is their age range? Are they single or are they married? Do they have children or don't they? If they do, how old are the children? The more detail you can provide, the better off you will be, because this information is used to sort through the wealth of available media and messaging options to pick those that will work best.

Research has demonstrated the applicability of Joseph Juran's 80/20 rule, also known as the Pareto Principle, to marketing. It says that in any given category, 80 percent of a product is bought by 20 percent of its consumers. These individuals are called heavy users.[1]

Therefore, most companies will begin by identifying these heavy users and designating them as the primary target. This makes perfect sense. A company's first priority should always be to maintain current customers, because retaining customers costs less than finding new ones. It is also easier to convince current customers to use a company's product or service more frequently, then it is to get a new customer. And finally, when a company does want to find new users, they are most likely similar in profile to current users.

Target heavy users for best results.

In some cases, advertisers may also want to identify niche targets (i.e. smaller, more well-defined segments) to address on a secondary basis. For example, the primary target for over-the-counter hemorrhoid products is Men, ages 45–60, who are overweight. But since 20–50 percent of pregnant women get hemorrhoids[2], it makes sense to run a smaller secondary campaign targeting Women 18–45, who are pregnant. Since these women can be reached very efficiently by a variety of targeted media, with low out-of-pocket costs, it is worth investing money in them, even if they will only use the product for a limited time.

Companies may also want to explore niche targets to see if these specialized groups can provide a growth opportunity. Typically, such efforts are driven by new research about either an underserved target market or the product/service.

For example, in 1993, while working on AT&T's business-to-business account, I came across an interesting piece of research that stated: "Women are starting small businesses at twice the rate of men, and they are expected to own over 40 percent of all small businesses by the year 2000."[3]

Using this fact, we recommended that AT&T look into directing a campaign toward the niche target of women starting their own businesses. They agreed that the idea had merit and funded the campaign. It was an unqualified success, generating both excellent public relations exposure and over 800 qualified leads.

Sometimes new information is discovered about a product/service that would make it appealing to a new niche target. For instance, a significant amount of research has been published recently about the health benefits of lydocane, which can be found in tomatoes. Currently, V8 targets Women 18 – 49 with children 1–12, using a broad health story. But what if V8 did a limited campaign targeting Men 50-65 with the simple message: "Drink V8 and live longer?" Might this not also be successful?[4]

Explore secondary niche targets to find new opportunities.

Ultimately, what will emerge from this approach to selecting target markets is a variety of target segments that will require entirely different communications plans and messaging. What makes this approach both possible and utterly necessary is the continued fragmentation of media, and the presence of various personality types in the population.

AT&T

A perfect example of company that does a terrific job targeting multiple niche segments is AT&T. In 2008/2009, the telecom company ran several different commercials, called pool-outs, based on the same strategy: "If you don't have AT&T, you might miss something important." One ad featured a teenaged Michael Phelps fan, another a mother of small children, still other spots featured people who travel on business, and men who try to cook.

The variety allowed AT&T to connect with a wide range of users and potential users with very targeted messaging. The media strategy was also tailored to the specific target niche, so the Phelp's Fan spot ran on MTV, while the mom spot ran on daytime soap operas.

Run multiple campaigns to address different market segments more effectively.

Chapter 3: Defining Target Markets

During the early 1980s, target markets were commonly defined as broadly as Adults 25–54. But think about that. That target includes you and your parents (or your kids). When was the last time you thought the same way as them about anything? And there's a reason why the book *Men are from Mars, Women are from Venus* was a best seller.[1] Men and women don't think alike either. My husband tells me I am a Plutonian.

The point is, the more clearly we can define who we are speaking to, the more likely it is that we will be able to communicate with them effectively.

The better job you do defining your target, the better your advertising will be.

Advertisers identify their audiences by looking at demographics and psychographics. Both of these are measures that divide the general population into smaller segments that will be easier to target.

Demographics

Typically we start by considering demographics, defined as: "Population or consumer statistics regarding socioeconomic factors such as age, income, sex, occupation, education, family size and the like."[2]

Below are some demographic areas you might want to consider when defining your target market. Please note that this list is meant to be a thought starter, rather than comprehensive.

Gender
Age
Marital status
Household income
Children
Education
Employment
Race

Geography
> Global
> National
> Regional
> Local
> Top cities

Including gender and a specific age range is mandatory when defining a target market. Most media is bought based on these parameters rather than total audience, so at the bare minimum they must be delineated.

Avoid definitions that are open to interpretation, such as "middle class." Instead, give a clear range, e.g. "Household income ranging from $40,000–$60,000." That way, all collaborators in the process will understand who they are trying to reach. This is particularly important since advertising is always created by committee; and these days, often remotely.

Psychographics

The next step is to define the target market's psychographics, i.e. "Criteria for segmenting consumers by lifestyle, attitudes, beliefs, values, personality, buying motives, and/or extent of product usage."[3]

Examples of psychographics include:
Hobbies
Sports
Religion
Culture
Personality traits
Product usage

Including psychographics as part of a well-defined target is important, because the addition of at least one specific criterion to gender and age range will provide enough direction to begin strategic development. It's easy to see that going from "Men 25–35" to "Men 25–35, who travel frequently on business" makes a huge difference in the way we would communicate with the target.

When defining targets, more criteria are better.

I once visited a company that had posted a Hockney-like portrait of its target, complete with textual information about her habits, likes, and dislikes, inspiring everyone working on the business. It was a great idea.

I sometimes ask my students to define a target market using ten demographic, two geographic, and ten psychographic criteria. It's once they get past the obvious traits and dig a little deeper that they discover the key differentiators that lead to true insights. That's why we should all take the time to clearly define our targets in great detail.

Tea Partay

In 2006, Smirnoff had the first YouTube smash hit with its *Tea Partay* two-minute rap parody for raw tea.[4] Interestingly, it is a detailed target definition from start to finish. Check it out. You'll learn everything about these folks from what they do for fun to how people feel about them.

Chapter 4: Consumer Insights

Research shows that we make purchase decisions based on emotional factors and then create rational reasons for what we have done.[1] For example, we may buy a Mercedes because it makes us feel important, and then tell ourselves that we purchased it because it's a good investment.

These findings can be applied directly to advertising as consumer insights— something the consumer thinks or feels that can be used to make an emotional connection with them.

While insights can be directly related to a product, the best ones generally aren't, because product-related issues don't tend to be emotional enough to create the connection we are seeking. For instance, it is fair to say that "People want to buy comfortable shoes." But, it would be difficult to build an emotional hook based on that fact.

On the other hand if we probe a bit deeper we can deduce that "People get angry when their shoes aren't comfortable." That approach opens up infinitely more possibilities to stir emotions.

Most purchase decisions are emotional.

Dove

In 2006, Dove began its much heralded, Effie award winning, *Real Beauty* campaign. The campaign, which features women who are not quite as perfect as those we typically see in mass communications, touched a nerve.

After its launch, the brand experienced two years of double-digit sales growth. The campaign strengthened brand loyalty among existing customers, resulting in a greater number of current users buying more than one product, and increased share growth in four of its five major categories.[2]

The consumer insight that led to its development was: "Only two percent of women consider themselves beautiful"— a fact that was uncovered in a worldwide survey. [3]

It took me two years before I tried a Dove product when I switched from bar soap, where I had an existing brand preference, to body wash. Since then, I've become a repeat customer. But, total Dove sales have since slowed, and the company has been tweaking its messaging in an effort to reestablish positive sales trends. [4]

Disney

Another example of using a consumer insight to connect with a target, albeit in a single execution, is the *Too Excited to Sleep* commercial that Disney aired in 2006/7. The ad which urges repeat visitors to return, uses the insight that many of us have difficulty sleeping when we are excited, to illustrate that the entire family is looking forward to their impending trip to Disneyworld.

Since I do not have children, I wasn't actually part of the intended target for this ad. So, the fact that I liked it and thought it was effective didn't really count, especially since I did not book a trip. But, while it was airing, I visited my brother, Ken Lehrer and his family, who are part of the target group depicted in the spot, and he informed me that they were going to Disneyworld. My response: "Six days, seven nights, $1500." He laughed. But clearly he found the ad motivating.

The following year, the commercial was revised and retargeted to first time visitors, another indication of its probable success.

Consumer insights that make an emotional connection with the target are the key to successful campaigns.

The previous two examples used consumer insights to develop superior creative executions. Advertisers can also use consumer insights to create more effective communication plans.

AT&T

The consumer insight for the AT&T effort that was targeted to female start-ups was that women entrepreneurs have a more difficult time raising capital than men. Based on this insight, a $50,000 start-up grant became the centerpiece for the communications plan. The contest was announced in *Working Women* magazine and both AT&T and co-sponsor Deloitte & Touche ran insertions urging women to enter.

Women were invited to send in their business plans, which were then evaluated by some volunteers from a local university. Based on their evaluation of the ideas, a winner was selected, and the award and grant money were presented at the annual National Association of Women Business Owners (NAWBO) meeting.

There is no doubt that the subsequent success of the campaign was because this incentive was perfectly suited to the needs of the target. By recognizing that fact, AT&T was essentially saying we understand you and we know how to help you, and we are going to work for you if you will let us.

Chapter 5: Research

My favorite former client, Doug Ritter, once said to me: "Don't show me any research. I can make research say whatever I want it to say!"

He's right, of course. Over the years, hundreds of magazine reps came to see me, and they all showed me research results indicating their publication was in the top three for reaching my target. They did it by dividing the data in a way that was to their advantage. This is often how research is used, and it defeats the very purpose of doing it. But, if research is approached properly, with an open mind, then it can be an invaluable aid in creating strong communications.

It's especially important when developing strategies to do a research check to make sure that the views you hold are consistent with those of the target market, since advertising personnel tend to be highly educated relative to the population at large and therefore biased in their assumptions.

Visa & Mastercard

In 1996, Visa ran a campaign with the tagline "It's everywhere you want to be." Each commercial featured a short description of a popular vacation destination/tourist attraction and ended with the thought that if you wanted to go there you needed a Visa card because they didn't accept American Express. Traveling is one of my passions, so this campaign really appealed to me. Even the commercials that featured places that didn't interest me were done with such panache that I found myself wanting to visit. In short, they pushed my travel button and hooked me.

At the time, I was working at McCann-Erickson as an account person on the global launch of Lucent Technologies. I was lucky enough to be collaborating with some of the finest creative talent in the business, including Joyce King Thomas, former CCO McCann New York and Jeroen Bours, CEO of Darling Advertising & Design. They were working on a new business pitch for Mastercard at the time, and Joyce shared the concept with me. My reaction was tepid, and I clearly remember saying "Gee Joyce, I don't know. I really think that Visa has nailed that strategy."

The campaign she described to me was of course the unparalleled, and much parodied, "Priceless" campaign, with its now familiar structure – Two tickets: $46. Two hotdogs, two popcorns, two sodas: $ 27. One autographed baseball: $50. Real conversation with 11-year-old son; Priceless." And the tagline, "There are some things money can't buy. For everything else, there's Mastercard."

How could I have been so silly? That's probably the best advertising campaign ever.

Think a minute about what it says—Money can buy happiness! Better yet—credit can buy happiness. That is certainly a much stronger promise than: You can go to cool places if you have this card. And when you consider how few Americans even have their passports (approximately 27 percent) versus how many are conspicuous consumers, it's pretty obvious why so many more have been motivated by the Mastercard strategy. [1]

Test your ideas to make sure that they resonate with your target.

There are two basic types of research – primary research, which is research the marketer does themselves and secondary research which is done by others and is available for purchase. It is always cheaper to buy secondary research then it is to field primary research, so we look at secondary research first to see if it can provide the needed information.

Secondary Research
Below are some secondary research sources that are available and the data that they supply.

- Demographic information: MRI (Mediamark Research & Intelligence) and Simmons focus mostly on consumer packaged goods and provide information about category and brand users across a wide variety of products and services.

- When telecom and technology accounts moved to the forefront in the early 1990s, Intelliquest emerged to provide similar information for those sectors.

- And more recently, Focalyst was introduced to provide in-depth information about Baby Boomers.

- Psychographic information: VALS and Prizm. The latter ties data directly to geographical segments, making it actionable.

- Consumer behavior information: Yankelovich and BrainReserve provide trend data about behavioral changes.

- Ratings data: A.C. Nielsen.

- Media information: TNS, LNA and SRDS.

It's important to note that ideas for new tactics often come from broader research, such as happiness studies or the news about the role of emotion in purchase decisions. This information can be found in general interest publications such as *The Wall Street Journal.*

Primary Research

Primary research is developed, fielded and analyzed by marketers. The most useful primary research is an attitude and usage (A&U) test. These are large omnibus studies covering a wide range of behaviors associated with the product/service, and its competitors. They tend to be very expensive so they are rarely done, but because they take a broad approach to uncovering new information, they are most likely to uncover insights that can significantly impact brands.

The least useful type of primary research is copy testing. Consumers are not creatives. They tend to be overwhelmed by executional details such as casting, music and storylines, which makes it difficult for them to judge strategies when they are shown completed advertisements. The better method for using research to enhance creative is to develop multiple positioning statements in text only format, let consumers pick their favorite strategy and then let the creatives do their thing.

There are two types of primary research—quantitative and qualitative.

Quantitative Research

In quantitative research, the sample size is statistically significant so the results can be accurately projected on a national basis. This not only means that the sample size will be large, it will also be geographically dispersed and include a representative mix of ages and races, and whatever other variables are relevant to the product category. Since the data will be tabulated to identify trends, questions are posed based on a five-point scale—i.e. totally agree, mostly agree, neutral, mostly disagree, and totally disagree.

Test concepts, not copy.

Country Inn Rice Dishes
In 1987, for the launch of Uncle Ben's Country Inn Rice Dishes, we used quantitative research to determine the best positioning for the product. We tested three strategies: The first described the brand as a combination of rice and vegetables, the second as an all-in-one meal and the third, spoke to the country inn heritage behind the recipes. It was the final idea that captured the targets' imagination. So much so, that we recommended the name of the line be changed to reflect that intelligence. The launch was a huge success, and the product line is still on the market today.

Recently, companies have begun combining research methodologies with modeling to provide comprehensive projections that start with awareness and end with sales volume projections. Along the way, the research provides information about everything from whether or not a particular scent is well received, to how quickly the marketer can expect users to repurchase.

Qualitative Research
Qualitative research, which mostly takes the form of focus groups or one-on-one interviews, is not statistically significant.

What researchers hear during a focus group, while always interesting, is not necessarily representative of what the majority of people think. For this reason, agencies usually schedule multiple groups with varying targets (e.g. users and non-users) in geographically dispersed cities.

When attending focus groups, one witnesses a wide variation in attitudes toward life in different places around the country. For instance, a few years ago we developed a campaign for Scotts Turf Builder that involved a couple taking care of their lawn together. In Cincinnati, Ohio the idea was met with disbelief and the resounding statement: "Lawns are men's work. Women belong in the kitchen." When the same creative was shared in a suburb of Philadelphia, the reaction was: "Well I don't know anything about lawns, so if she wants to help out, good for her."

Clearly we were dealing with two very different targets and needed separate messaging in order to properly address their mindsets. In fact, I have never been to a focus group where I didn't learn something that led to a new idea. Talking to consumers usually has that effect; we just need to be careful how we interpret what we hear.

Talk to your customers and let them teach you.

Online Testing

Another form of research that is growing in popularity is online testing, which appears to provide results that are at least as good as offline research, and maybe even better. Not only is it faster and less expensive than traditional qualitative testing, it also eliminates group think, which is an issue that often arises in focus groups, where one articulate person can sway the others in a room.

One caveat is that the stimuli used in online testing can greatly influence the results, with more finished presentations yielding stronger results.

Chapter 6: Advertising Strategy Recommendation

This chapter provides an example of an advertising strategy recommendation that is similar to the ones created by advertising practitioners today. It incorporates all the information discussed in the previous five chapters.

The purpose of this particular strategy recommendation is to recommend a new niche market for an existing product or service. Ideas such as this come from research that tells us something new about either consumers or the product/service. My inspiration for this example came from a taxi top ad that said: Guinness – 90 calories.

Strategic Advertising Recommendation: Guinness

We recommend that Guinness implement a niche advertising plan targeting Women 21–30, who are counting calories but still like to have fun.

Background
While current advertising for Guinness is gender-neutral, the company's Web site focuses on the core beer drinker, Men 21–30. While this group continues to show a preference for beer over wine and spirits, category sales are expected to grow at a disappointing two percent rate over the next five years. ("US Beer Industry", 2008)

A new entry into the beer category -- MGD 64, highlights the calorie count of beer versus other types of alcohol in its advertising campaign, which targets females. A 12-ounce glass of Guinness contains 125 calories. But, it has twice as much alcohol as MGD 64 and is exceptionally filling.

Recommendation/Rationale

We recommend that Guinness implement the "Girl's Night Out" campaign, targeted to Women 21–30. It will focus on the low-calorie/more satisfying qualities of the drink.

This recommendation is based on the following rationale:

1. Women currently account for 25 percent of beer consumption in the United States, and they are a growing market. ("Women and Beer Fact Versus Fiction", 2009). Since there are approximately 20 million women in the United States between the ages of 21 and 30, they represent an opportunity for Guinness to increase sales beyond the predicted meager growth rates. ("Population estimates", 2009)

2. Most women currently believe beer contains far more calories than it actually does. Since 67 percent of women report they are trying to lose weight, simply informing them that a 12-ounce glass of Guinness has 125 calories could yield very dramatic results. (Clark-Flory, 2008) Despite its calorie count being twice as high as MGD 64, we believe

women will recognize that Guinness's extra alcohol and more filling quality make it the better choice.

3. The "Girl's Night Out" campaign taps into social trends and reaches out to women while they party. It makes extensive use of social media, on-site collateral, and sampling to encourage further word-of-mouth activities. It will be a highly effective and efficient effort.

Program Details

This campaign will take place in bars in selected cities. Efforts will focus on major population centers and cities with a high percentage of Women 21–30, such as university towns.

Invitations to related events will be sent virally using social media, popular blogs, YouTube, and Facebook fan pages. The bars will be specially decorated with banners, posters, tablecloths, and postcards.

All women present at the event will receive one free glass of Guinness. The event will include games, with T-shirts and other branded items for prizes. Participants will be encouraged to record the festivities and post the videos on their social networks. They will also be invited to opt-in to an e-mail list that will distribute coupons for in-store purchases and invitations to future events.

Next Steps

Pending agreement to the overall direction of the plan, we will develop specific budget recommendations and select cities and venues to target. We would like to reach an agreement within the next week, so we can implement it in the fall.

(2008) US Beer Industry Posts second Consecutive Year of Case Sales Gains. *redorbit.com*. Retrived, June 2, 2009 from http://www.redorbit.com/news/business/1580606/us_beer_industry_posts_second_co nsecutive_year_of_case_sales/

(2009) Women and Beer: Fact Versus Fiction. *drinkfocus.com*. Retrived, June 2, 2009 from http://www.drinkfocus.com/articles/beer/women-and-beer.php

(2009, May 14) Population estimates. *US Census Bureau*. Retrived, June 4, 2009 from http://www.census.gov/popest/national/asrh/NC-EST2008/NC-EST2008-01.xls

Clark-Flory, T. (2008, April 25) Study: Most women "disordered eaters". *Self Magazine*. Retrived, June 14, 2009 from http://www.salon.com/mwt/broadsheet/2008/04/25/eating/

Part II: Communications Planning

Chapter 7: Television

In 2009, several studies confirmed that television advertising is still the most effective way to reach broad audiences and may be more effective now than it was prior to the media explosion of the 1990s.[1]

Network Television

Currently, there are five national broadcast networks in the U.S.: ABC, CBS, NBC, Fox, and CW. Airtime can be bought across the country on these networks, which run in every television market, and therefore have the potential to reach 114.9 million households. [2] Because of this, network television is defined as a high reach medium.

But, the audience that it reaches is comprised of a wide variety of people across all demographic and psychographic measures. We have already discussed the fact that the heavy users for most products and services are a small portion of the total population. Therefore, depending upon the size of the actual target market, advertising on network television could entail wasting a good deal of money advertising to people who are not part of the group.

Network television can be expensive. Since costs in advertising are based primarily on the number of people who will see the effort, and network television delivers large audiences, it is priced accordingly. Shows that deliver the most people run in prime time, which is defined as Monday – Friday 8:00 p.m. – 11:00 p.m.

In 2010, the finale of *American Idol* drew an estimated 24 million viewers. [3] Lower rated shows, draw fewer viewers. Likewise, less watched dayparts such as daytime and early morning have smaller audiences, and lower ratings.

Pricing is aligned with viewership. The cost for running a commercial on that finale was $490,000. [4] And, while the cost for running commercials on daytime and early morning shows would be proportionately less, network television is usually a costly medium when one factors in the expensive of running an adequate number of spots and producing a commercial.

What would be considered a typical low-end schedule for a quarter of national advertising—a combination of thirty-and fifteen-second spots running on cable and syndicated programs during the daytime and weekends—costs about $3 million.

The broadest reach medium is a sub-segment of primetime television referred to as marquee prime. The leader of the bunch is *The Super Bowl*, which has been known to bring in as many as 900 million viewers and charge advertisers $2 million to communicate with them. Of course since *The Super Bowl* garners so much attention and free publicity, it is in a class of its own. Other highly-rated marquee shows include *The Academy Awards* and *The Olympics*.

Here is a list of television dayparts and their time frames:

- Early Morning   6 a.m. – 12 p.m.
- Daytime   1 p.m. – 5 p.m.
- Early Fringe   6 p.m. – 8 p.m.
- Evening News   6 p.m. – 7 p.m.
- Prime   8 p.m. – 11 p.m.
- Late Fringe/Late News   11 p.m. – 12 a.m.
- Late Night   12 a.m. – 6 a.m.
- Sunday Morning News   7 a.m. – 12 p.m.
- Weekend   1 p.m. – 11 p.m.
- Sports (Weekends)   1 p.m. – 8:00 p.m.

Cable Television

In addition to the national broadcast networks, the U.S. has numerous cable networks that are carried in select television markets. The reach of each cable network is limited by the amount of homes in which it is available. That availability depends not only upon where the networks are carried, but also whether subscribers are willing to pay a fee to view them.

The cable networks with the broadest reach, charge carriers low fees, and generally are included in basic cable packages which maximize their reach. Examples of these cable networks are TNT and TBS. Not coincidently, they also carry a wide range of programming designed to reach a large audience, much as the national networks do.

Most cable networks take a more targeted approach, limiting their programming to attract a specific audience. This works well since most advertisers only want to reach a specific audience segment. As a result, some cable advertising costs have gone up significantly in the past few years, even though they are not necessarily delivering larger audiences. Advertisers are willing to pay more for these stations as they deliver more qualified prospects.

Examples of these types of cable networks include: HGTV, whose focus on the home attracts viewers who may be renovating or decorating their own homes; Food network, which as the name implies appeals to chefs and wanna be's; and the Disney channel, which attracts children in abundance.

Since cable television reaches fewer viewers, prices are lowered accordingly.

Syndication
Examples of syndicated television include *Wheel of Fortune* and *The Dr. Oz Show*. While these programs may ultimately run in most markets, they don't necessarily appear at the same time or on the same network affiliate in every market. Therefore, they are often purchased on a local basis rather than a national one. Nationally, since they deliver smaller audiences than network, they too cost less.

Syndicated shows have come up with many clever ways to attract low budget advertisers such as product placement, sponsoring of closed-captioning, and ten-second IDs.

Spot Television

It is possible to buy television time on a local basis rather than a national basis. Typically each half-hour show that runs on network television reserves several minutes of advertising to be sold on a local basis. This enables advertisers to not only buy single markets, but also just a few markets, depending upon their needs.

If production costs can be kept down, then local advertisers can employ cable networks in individual markets at a relatively low cost and harness the power of television on a smaller scale.

Barkinglot

Barkinglot, a doggie daycare company, paid $299 to create its ad and purchased $1,400 in ad time, which allowed its ad to run 144 times over a two-week period on Chicago cable systems. Customer phone calls jumped by 20 percent during those two weeks.[5]

Video News Releases (VNRs)

VNRs are short pieces of content produced by advertisers, which are placed on news shows free of charge. The information has to be deemed news worthy by the media that incorporates it. But, assuming it has been, this can be a very inexpensive way to garner air time without incurring significant costs.

Television Buying
There are three methods for buying network television: upfront, scatter, and opportunistic.

Big advertisers, who spend money in all four quarters of the year, will participate in the upfront market in order to lock in the best programs and prices. They buy packages, which allow the networks to sell their lower rated shows along with their stars. They are guaranteed that the packages they buy will deliver the specified audience. If it does not, they will be compensated with make-goods – additional airings that allow the commercial to achieve its planned delivery.

Advertisers who do not run advertising throughout the year buy their weight quarterly in the scatter market. Typically they will pay higher rates than those who purchased during the upfront. Delivery is not guaranteed, although make-goods for under delivery are usually still the norm.

While most will buy packages as those in the upfront do, others will employ an alternative approach called cherry-picking. These advertisers will pay a premium to be on a particular show. Often these are higher rated shows, which tend to attract light television viewers. While these individuals may not view advertising often, they make an appointment to watch these favorites, and often do so with friends.

The final buying method is called opportunistic. As the name implies this method involves taking advantage of inventory imbalances. When networks have inventory that they have not sold in the upfront and scatter markets that they do not need to use for make-good purposes, they are willing to lower prices to sell the inventory. (They also sometimes run advertisements for other programming that they carry.)

Opportunistic buying works best if the product being sold has little or no seasonality since there are no guarantees that inventory will be available at any given time.

One brand that makes great use of the method is Preparation H. The primary target for the brand is Men 45-60 and sales occur fairly evenly throughout the year. Prep H allocates some of its yearly television budget to opportunistically buy time during sporting events that run into overtime. The networks cannot sell this time in advance since it may not occur. And, viewership tends to rise when a game goes into overtime. So, it's a terrific opportunity.

Don't automatically rule out television based on expense.

Chapter 8: Radio

Radio is the medium that doesn't get any respect. It deserves better. 77% of adults are reached by broadcast radio on a daily basis; and almost 80% of 18-34 year-olds listen to broadcast radio on an average day. [1]

Research shows that radio retains 92% of its listeners during commercial breaks.[2] Perhaps it is because radio is primarily a local medium and messages are frequently promotional in nature.

Radio audiences are increasing despite the availability of so many other musical alternatives. Stations tend to limit their programming to attract a highly targeted audience, which is very appealing to advertisers seeking specific segments.

Production costs are low, and can even be non-existent if a company chooses to have a live announcer read their copy. This facilitates the ability to do tailored creative for different markets.

Typically ads are :60 seconds in length. The rationale is that the extra copy is needed to compensate for the lack of a visual.

Don't forget about radio – especially if you are a local advertiser.

Chapter 9: Print

While there is little doubt that video trumps print as consumers' favored method for information delivery, and that everything that can move to video eventually will, print vehicles may still have a future.[1]

Magazines

Gen X and Gen Y read more magazines per month than Baby Boomers and the Silent Generation. Specifically, a 2007 study shows that 19–24 year-olds reported reading an average of 18.3 titles during the previous six months. Likewise, 25–34 year-olds read 18.9 magazines, while those aged 45–54 read 16.7 titles, and people over 65 read 14.[2]

At this time, national magazines remain a terrific way to continuously reach an audience if you have $3–$5 million a year to spend. Because magazines are seldom read by only one person, reach is built slowly as the book is passed from reader to reader. It generally takes about three months for a monthly magazine to reach its full circulation, which makes it an ideal vehicle for creating a low level of sustained buzz.[3]

These days, experimentation abounds as advertisers try to maximize the value of their magazine plans. They run a variety of interesting inserts, including ones that pop up, sing, and smell and taste good.[4] And, embedded bar codes and text messages are turning print ads into gateways to additional mobile and online efforts.[5] Some publications, such as *Lucky,* are even fully dedicated to sales.

Placing ads next to relevant editorial increases the chance the ad will be seen by readers interested in the advertisers' product. While magazines once worried inordinately about editorial integrity and the separation between advertising and editorial, those lines have begun to blur and the result is the availability of better editorial adjacencies. For example, *Relish* magazine recently followed an article about an artesian olive oil company with an ad for an olive oil can. It was a fractional ad, which typically gets less attention than a full-page ad, but it was hard to miss, given the location of its placement.[6]

Some magazines also provide highly targeted audiences, which makes them a terrific medium. Readers of *Travel & Leisure* are likely to be interested in travel and may even be planning a vacation. For agencies placing ads for overseas resorts, this is a great publication to run in, because it is unlikely that they will waste money advertising to people who might not even have passports.

Magazines also dedicate certain issues to specific topics, which increases the chances of getting more bang for your buck. For example, an issue of *Travel & Leisure* that features the Caribbean will be a great place for a hotel located in that region to advertise.

Finally, magazines have been making great strides in moving the product online, with digital traffic increasing 11 percent in the fourth quarter of 2008.[7] And they are poised to make the move to mobile devices as soon as technology allows.[8]

Magazines can provide broad continuous reach.

Newspapers
Newspapers are a bit trickier. I asked a class of undergrads if they read newspapers, and they responded: "Only when someone leaves them on the seat on the train." Not very encouraging. They also complained about the tendency of newsprint to get on their hands.

Newspapers have been bleeding for years as their primary source of income— classified ads—have been completely usurped by Web sites such as craigslist.com, and careerbuilder.com. At the same, time many retail advertisers, like Macy's, are moving spending to television, at the expense of newspapers and radio.

A survey of paid circulation trends as of September 2008 indicates that only five of the top twenty-five newspapers showed increases versus 1990: *The Wall Street Journal, USA Today, The New York Post, The Houston Chronicle*, and *The Arizona Republic*, which was up an astonishing 9.26 percent.[9]

Newspapers have been slow to move online and are now struggling to regain lost ground. Some won't make it. The venerable *Rocky Mountain News* officially folded on February 26, 2009, after 150 years.[10]

But, in the short run, the tightening of newspapers' target market, which now consists of mostly older, wealthier, and more educated males, provides a very attractive market for products aimed at affluent Baby Boomers.

And, *The Arizona Republic* which has been successful because of its focus on the Sunday paper provides a clue about how the media can maintain its relevance going forward.[11]

For the right audience, newspapers can be a smart buy.

Chapter 10: Out-Of-Home (OOH)

Out of Home

Out-of-Home (OOH) advertising is the second fastest growing medium after the Internet.[1] Advertisers have always valued outdoor for its ability to deliver mass audiences, and now it is particularly valuable since television is less able to consistently reach mass audiences.

The primary issue advertisers have with OOH is the long lead times it requires, typically six months at a minimum. Other issues include time-run commitments, which are generally for at least a month, and the inability to make creative changes during a run.

The move to digital billboards is erasing all these concerns, and will lead to an explosion in the medium. Digital billboards can be developed more quickly, don't require months for printing, can be changed frequently, and they can even be interactive. The ability to change copy based on time of day allows advertisers to tailor messages. For example, a fast food chain can run ads for breakfast sandwiches in the morning and burgers in the afternoon. And a billboard in Chicago's O'Hare airport is testing creative that changes languages based on where the arriving flight originated.[2]

Interactive digital advertising can also include text messages and bar codes that viewers can access for more information, contests, and downloads, as well as plug-in boxes that allow people to use their headphones to sample songs and kiosks with touch screens.

My favorite application is interactive kiosks at bus stops, which were tested in London in 2006.[3] The kiosks provided local area maps so people could locate neighborhood stores when they got off the bus. This was a win-win for local merchants and consumers. I can't wait for them to come to New York City. My classes thought the kiosks would work great outside subway stations too.

The real future for out-of-home digital advertising is video. Just go to Times Square and look around; it is easy to see that what catches the eye most is video. We already see video in stores, elevators, gas stations, and bus kiosks, and recently, I saw my first video ad on the side of a bus. Since most of these formats require visuals that communicate without words, they provide an interesting creative challenge that advertisers need to master.

Digital and video out-of-home are ripe for innovation.

Chapter 11: Internet

It didn't take a marketing genius to figure out the Internet would change everything. The question was "How?" The answer is ever-evolving.

While the Internet gives consumers more control over the information they receive, that control doesn't mean they no longer want any information. In fact, consumers crave information more now as options continue to proliferate. And the Web's ability to overcome geographical separation has opened up a wider array of purchase opportunities, globally.

Internet Searches

When someone seeks information on the Internet, he uses a search engine—most likely Goggle—to find it.[1] Therefore, search engine optimization is a must in today's world. The basic methodologies for SEO are term repetition, meta code and increasing links. The first two relate to the fact that most search programs are designed to look for the specific words that have been used in the search. Therefore repeating these words numerous times, will allow the site to emerge higher on the list. With meta code, this repetition is done behind the scenes. Increasing links involves getting your site mentioned on other sites with links back to your site. In a sense they are just another method of increasing repetition.

Advertisers also have the option to buy keywords. This can be an effective way to reach more consumers, but marketers need to closely track the performance of the words they buy all the way through to purchase to ensure their money is being spent as effectively as possible. A client of mine, Admento, makes Lucite promotional items. When we reviewed his Internet traffic patterns, we found that while the key word trophies garnered many clicks, those clicks generated few sales because searchers were most likely looking for traditional cups and plaques. Therefore, it made financial sense for him to drop the word.

In 1996, Yahoo and Google began offering local search packages with some intriguing results. The packages, which included a detailed Web page linked to the search ad, cost from $250 to $300 a month. Results released in a case study for a local Philadelphia hair salon indicated that Web site hits increased from 20,000 per quarter to 280,000.[2]

Sponsored searches are a great way to connect directly with information seekers.

Web sites

In many cases, when a consumer uses a search engine, he is looking for the brand's Web site. This is a tremendous opportunity for companies. The consumer is actually coming to them in search of information. All brands need to do is supply it. However, many fail to capitalize on this opportunity. A good Web site is expensive. It takes imagination and many

hours of labor to both build and maintain. It requires the input of cross-functional teams and outside experts. But if it's done correctly, it will be worth it.

Eventually, all Web sites will predominately feature video. As discussed previously, video is the preferred form of communication for consumers, and as the technology to both produce and deliver video continues to advance, it will become more prevalent. Additions of informational videos to Web sites have generated positive results. After posting consumer friendly how-to videos in 2008, Circuit City reported increases in loyalty, conversions, and revenue; including a 12-percent increase in some accessory sales.[3]

Nike+

My favorite example of "best use of Web site" at time of publication is Nike+. The Nike+ program was developed to reach elite runners who tended not to be Nike customers. This is how it works: A small sensor is placed in runners' shoes to transmit information about their runs, such as distance covered, distance remaining, pace, and calories burned to their iPods. The information is then conveyed verbally through the iPod to runners as they run, along with inspirational tunes of their choice.

Afterward, runners can upload the information to Nike's Web site where they can analyze, chart, and share it with other runners, thus creating a virtual community. Runners can also

post their times, challenge other participants, and form running teams.[4] Initial results indicated that on average, runners visited the site three times a week. And, a global race in 2009 was expected to attract 780,000 runners.[5]

Nike has also been creating local running clubs in conjunction with the online program that help members map out running routes, provide training advice, sponsor free evening speaker series, and organize group runs. The goal is to endear people to the brand and provide opportunities for them to try new products.[6]

Make your Web site the hub of marketing activities to optimize results.

People want to purchase things online, but many Web sites are still struggling to handle transactions well. Among those who have mastered the basics, the next challenge is to increase the breadth of their offers. Virtual stores allow for far more inventory than brick-and-mortar ones, yet few retailers capitalize on this online.

One retailer that has is Neiman Marcus, which now offers a far wider selection of handbags online than in stores. Saks Fifth Avenue offers different merchandise online versus in store, which is targeted to a younger shopper than the typical in-store customer. And mid-price chains such as JC Penny are experimenting with premium-priced items that are sold exclusively online.[7]

Your online inventory should be more robust than offline.

However, many techniques currently being used to engage consumers have yet to prove their worth in terms of sales generation. Many enjoyed the "period" sitcoms that Dove Night ran, where they placed their spokesperson Felicity Huffman in classics like *The Munsters*, but never bought their products, or even signed up for their free samples. And I know of at least one person who competed in the Heinz consumer-generated ad contest that only bought one bottle of the product—the one he used in the ad. And, while I applauded the creativity of Brawny paper towels' manly website, how much of a relationship do I need to have with my paper towels?

Don't mistake engagement for purchase intent.

Mobile Devices
A January 2008 Deloitte & Touche study found that 36 percent of people reported using their cell phones for entertainment purposes, up 12 percent from spring 2007.[8] And, in January 2009, 63.2 million people reported accessing news and

information on their mobile devices daily, which was twice as many as the previous year.[9]

As mobile technology improves, an increasing number of people will access the Web primarily through mobile devices. So, marketers will benefit from considering what their sites can deliver via this medium and create additional content, if necessary.

Mobile Internet usage will become a part of people's daily lives.

Email
Communicating one-to-one via the Internet has opened a new range of possibilities for marketers. The industry has embraced email marketing with 80 percent of marketers identifying it as their most effective means of advertising.[10]

Email marketing can be even more effective if marketers tailor their efforts according to the target's preferences. While Amazon has always done a terrific job with its "Based on your purchase, you might like this…" approach, sadly, no one else has used this approach effectively. In fact, most of the emails I receive remain outwardly focused, i.e. "This is what we have on sale this week…" Too bad. I usually stop looking at those companies' emails once I realize they have no connection to my buying patterns. What a tremendous waste of a golden opportunity.

Customize your email marketing to get better results.

Online Advertising

Who doesn't love the instant feedback that tracking Internet clicks provides? But, I am not yet convinced of the value of random banners, boxes, pop-ups, pre-rolls, and other forms of online advertising. Perhaps this is because my only goal when faced with these is to ignore them and disengage as quickly as possible, usually without even noticing what is being advertised.

While most marketers share my behavior patterns, they believe younger audiences are different. Yet, my undergrad students say they ignore everything on the perimeter of the pages they view, and that this behavior carries over into other media.

However, I recently saw an online ad that I did read. While a page from *nytimes.com* was printing, an ad popped up in the corner of the screen that said "Printable version sponsored by…" Since I was on-hold anyway, I welcomed the opportunity to view the ad.

Contextual targeting, which matches ads with the content on viewer's screen, is a step in the right direction toward making ads more relevant to readers. And, we know that increasing relevance increases both attention and results.[11] Perhaps when we reach the point where we only deliver relevant ads, then people will choose to read them.

Increase relevance of online advertising to improve results.

Social Networking

YouTube

While Smirnoff's *Tea Partay* is acknowledged to be YouTube's first smash hit, the clip that really got advertisers to sit up and take notice of online's potential was Dove's *Evolution* ad. The 75-second spot, which demonstrates the lengths that make-up artists, hairdressers, and even retouchers, go through to create the photos we see on billboards, was brilliant. The spot won top honors in both the Cyber and Film categories at The Cannes Film Festival in 2007, the first execution to do so.[12]

The execution, which cost $150,000 to produce[13], generated approximately 270 million impressions on Dove's *Real Beauty* Web site—that's three times the amount generated by Dove's *Super Bowl* ad, which cost $2 million to run. The trade press headline "Better ROI from YouTube Video Than Super Bowl Spot" was a real attention grabber.[14] Oddly enough though, no one else has been able to capture that magic since, and when Dove tried again they failed.

In the meantime, social networking has taken off and Facebook, Twitter, MySpace, and LinkedIn have all increased their user bases.[15] But, attempts to actually make money from them have been less than successful. Simply using the same advertising formats within social media that have been used with other media doesn't seem to be working, so out-of-the-box thinking may be required, although a recent study suggests that once again the primary issue is advertising relevance, or lack thereof.[16]

New media may require new advertising formats.

Chapter 12: Communications Strategies

The way we approach communications planning has changed a great deal since the 1980s. This is because advertising campaigns have shifted their focus from mass media to targeted media and integrated marketing communications (IMC) plans.

Mass Media → *Integrated Marketing Communications*

There are three key reasons for this change:

1. More targeted media options

Believe it or not, in the early 1980s, cable channels were a tough sell. Advertisers were convinced that mass audiences were the best way to build their businesses, and those audiences watched network television.

But, as advertisers realized the target they were most interested in reaching—their heavy users—were a smaller, better-defined group, the appeal of more targeted media grew. If a close match could be made between target and media, then fewer dollars would be "wasted" on people who weren't actually part of the target audience. For example, it's a pretty sure bet that most people watching HGTV have an interest in homes. So, if you are selling paint, HGTV is probably a place you want to be. Since you will reach more people who want to paint, and fewer who don't then you would on a network such as ABC.

Use targeted media to reach your audience more efficiently.

The Internet accelerated these trends because of its ability to reach highly specific target groups. For example, when you can reach thousands of synchronized swimmers who burn through a half dozen bathing suits each year by running a very low out-of-pocket effort on <u>www.usasynchro.org</u>, why would you bother spending significantly more on a daytime television spot that probably reaches fewer swimmers and many more couch potatoes?

The trend toward more targeted media appears likely to continue, since it better meets the needs of both advertisers and consumers. In early 2009, *Parenting* magazine announced that it was splitting the publication into two: *Parenting Early Years* and *Parenting School Years*. It's pretty obvious that the diaper companies and the school supplies distributors will both be delighted with the change. And, the parents will too. It's definitely a win-win situation.

TD Bank
A nice example of a targeted IMC plan was the 2007 re-launch of Commerce Bank as TD Bank. Maintaining the positioning used by Commerce: "We're doing anything that makes people's lives more convenient," TD demonstrated that same strategy by using a variety of tactics, including:

- "At your convenience" sweepstakes, with prizes such as a personal chef, housecleaner, or chauffeur-driven limo to and from work for a week
- "Random acts of convenience" such as: free cups of coffee and TD-branded umbrellas
- "Random partner actions" such as: free dry cleaning and free pizza delivery
- "Holiday tie-ins" such as: gift-wrapping, shopping advice, and branded shopping bags at local malls and on Yahoo Shopping Online Gift Finder

Other branding initiatives included television commercials featuring Regis & Kelly, newspaper ads, and blanketing train stations with advertisements.[1]

2. The realization that one type of media does not fit everyone

Advertising has been around since 150 B.C. when the Romans used posters to promote candidates for Senate.[2] Most marketers had no problem creating their own print materials and signs, and did so for many years. Some still do so today.

Advertising agencies were created with the advent of television because clients lacked the expertise necessary to develop commercials in-house. The media planning process was developed to suit the needs of the pioneers—packaged goods companies, in particular Procter & Gamble and General Foods.

Based on available communications research, this process was developed: First achieve the minimum-spending threshold necessary to communicate properly in television, and then use any leftover money to augment the plan with print.

As a light television viewer, I have to admit this approach never made sense to me. Typically, when an individual is a light user of one medium, he is a heavy user of a different one. So, intuitively it makes sense to use multiple types of media to reach a broader range of people. Research supports this hypothesis. It also suggests that multi-media campaigns are more effective at achieving conversion.[3]

The use of multiple forms of media increases reach and effectiveness.

3. A need for greater impact

Due in part to the ever-increasing fragmentation of media, the average American city dweller sees up to an estimated 5,000 ads per day.[4] Not surprisingly, we have developed very sophisticated techniques for ignoring most of them. Therefore, advertisers are always seeking ways to increase the impact of their ads.

Integrated plans that include a "wow" tactic, which speaks to the target, are more likely to be seen. It stands to reason that if you appeal to someone's interests, whether it be creating their own commercials or "elfing" themselves, they won't filter you out. The tricky part is to make sure the link between the plan and the product is strong enough to fulfill the primary mission of making people want to buy something. While many of us, myself included, chuckled at the dancing elves we were sent, how many even noticed who sponsored them?[5]

Campbell's

To increase impact for their heart healthy products, Campbell's participated in the American Heart Association's Go Red campaign in a way that directly tied heart health to the company's products, resulting in increased product awareness and sales.[6]

The campaign debuted in February 2008, with a unique approach to product placement. Campbell's struck a deal with ABC daytime that encompassed three popular soap operas and the talk show *The View*. Significant heart-related storylines were incorporated into each soap, along with such overly blatant product placements that I was initially taken aback, and reminded of the movie *The Truman Show*.

The soap opera stars also delivered public service announcements about the dangers of heart disease for women at the end of their shows and directed viewers to Campbell's Web site for more information. *The View*'s hosts wore red on a specified day, and discussed the topic as one of the show's issues du jour.

TV efforts were augmented with a dedicated microsite www.campbellsaddressyourheart.com. The site engages consumers with polls, contests, medical information, promotional items for sale, an opportunity to make donations for research, and, of course, information about Campbell's heart-healthy products.

Product Placement

Given the increasing penetration of digital video recorders (DVRs)—27 percent of American households and 63 percent of households with an annual income of $100,000 or greater use the devices[7] —I believe that direct product placement is the future of television advertising. It will be understood that any item pictured in a show may be purchased. Viewers will see something they want to buy, pause the program, make their purchase, and then return to the show where they left off. In 2009, Cablevision began experimenting with the technique in Long Island, NY and Connecticut.

Include a "wow" tactic in your integrated campaign to cut through the clutter.

Chapter 13: Objectives, Strategies & Tactics

Once we clearly understand our target and have identified a meaningful consumer insight, we can use this information, combined with our product/service knowledge, to sort through the available media options and arrive at an optimal communications plan.

It is imperative to get buy-in for the communications strategy prior to planning, because the overwhelming wealth of media options now available means the iterations are infinite, and without an agreed-to strategy, it is impossible to evaluate which are most appropriate.

Typically, media strategies are communicated in three steps: objectives, strategies, and tactics.

Product/Service + Target/Insight → Communication Objectives → Communication Strategies → Communication Tactics

These steps are defined as follows:

Communications Objectives
What is the goal for the campaign? What are you hoping the media will accomplish?

Communications Strategies

How will you achieve your objectives? What media will you use?

Communications Tactics

How will you use that media? What are the specifics? What is your "wow" tactic?

Dockers

One interesting example of an integrated campaign was Dockers' effort for Father's Day 2007. The stated goal was to own Father's Day. The "wow" tactic was a microsite that invited consumers to share tribute stories and photos of their fathers, which were then broadcast on the Reuters news board in New York's Times Square from 12–2 p.m., June 12–16, with a 20-hour Dockers-only stream on Father's Day, June 17. The wearing of Docker's by participants was optional.

The effort was accompanied by print, television, radio, and online support.[1]

Examples

Following are three simplified examples created to demonstrate the desired connection between consumer insight and communications strategy.

Example 1: Supplemental disability insurance (SDI)

Product/Service
Supplemental disability insurance provides additional income when people are unable to work due to illness or accident.

Target
Men 25–49, married with children under 16, and household incomes of $50,000 - $100,000.

Insight
They are very involved parents.

Objective
Schedule 100 meetings per region in the next 6 months.

Strategy
- Partner with local Boy and Girl Scout organizations.
- Use online media and events to efficiently reach the target.

Tactics
- Facilitate booths that provide safety tips and information about SDI at Girl and Boy Scout picnics.
- Sponsor monthly email newsletters about the scouts, which include safety tips sponsored by SDI.
- Sponsor a parent/child "Habitat for Humanity" event.

Example 2: Computer Brand A

Product
Computers

Target
Men 16–24, who are computer nerds.

Insight
They love gaming.

Objective
Increase sales for Computer Brand A by ten percent.

Strategy
Team up with the NBC sit-com, *Chuck*.

Tactics
- Create a massively multiplayer online game (MMOG) based on the *Chuck* series.
- Promote the game on the television show via product placement and commercials, as well as in a microsite on the computer brand's website.
- Offer a guest appearance on *Chuck* as the grand prize.

Example 3: Plant fertilizer B

<u>Product</u>
A line of plant fertilizer products.

<u>Target</u>
The target is Women 35 – 55, who are active gardeners.

<u>Insight</u>
They have a tremendous passion for gardening, and love to share their knowledge with others.

<u>Objective</u>
Increase awareness of the Plant Fertilizer B by 20% among Women 35-55 who are plant mavens, to increase product buzz.

<u>Strategy</u>
- Sponsor a seasonal best gardener contest.
- Promote the contest in *Better Homes & Gardens* and on the *Today Show*.

<u>Tactics</u>
- Announce the contest with an event; publicize it in gardening magazines and websites.
- Partner with *Better Homes & Gardens* and the *Today Show* for launch publicity, ongoing updates and announcement of the winner.

- Create and distribute a weekly highlights email.

Use consumer insights to create more effective communications plans

Chapter 14: Communications Planning

Once the strategy is agreed to, planning begins. Almost as soon as computers graduated from punch cards to WYSIWYG (circa 1980) agencies began using them to provide models for optimizing media planning efforts.

The earliest computer models were based on fairly crude measurements of the percentage of people who would see the ad (reach) and the average number of times those people would see it (frequency). As computers have advanced, so too has modeling, and these days every media agency has its own proprietary model that it employs on its clients' behalf.

Reach and Frequency
The goal of most media plans is to reach as many people as possible in the target as efficiently as possible. But, since repetition is a key component of learning it is the first factor that must be considered.

The Rule of Threes says that consumers need to see an ad three times before they act on it. Thus, the minimum effective frequency for any piece of communication is set at three.[1]

In fact, there is a rich history to the Rule of Threes. People remember things in groups of three. That's why our phone numbers are arranged in groups of three.[2] Many studies have been conducted to ascertain why. Researchers generally believe that it is tied to our ability to see patterns and that three is the smallest set size that allows us to do so.

Bear in mind that while a campaign may deliver an average frequency of three, heavy viewers of a medium will see the ad more times and light viewers will see it fewer. Quintile analyses, which break down frequency based on viewer media habits, are used to ascertain when the ad achieves wear-out—the point where people no longer bother to watch it. This is generally in the five–eight exposure range, although factors such as the ad's likeability and whether or not it is taken off air periodically, can greatly affect this number.[3]

In fact, advertising modeling systems have demonstrated that effectiveness of creative is so integral to determining adequate spending levels and optimal media plans, that companies such as Procter & Gamble, who for many years gave little thought to the quality of its creative, now send personnel to the Cannes Advertising Award Show to study how to improve it.[4]

Based on my own observation, current models do not appear to adequately account for significantly different viewing patterns between targeted media and more general media. Although I am, by definition, a light television viewer—the average American watched five hours of television daily during the fourth quarter of 2008[5]—I am an avid gardener who will watch HGTV's gardening block on rainy Sunday mornings.

During three hours of viewing, I am sometimes exposed to a commercial more than six times, i.e., more than once per half-hour show; more than twice the necessary amount. Those advertisers would be better served by capping their frequency and extending their reach through additional media.

Avoid overly heavy frequency.

Impressions/CPMs

Media is generally priced based on the amount of people who see it; each viewing is called an impression. These raw numbers tend to get large rather quickly. So, advertising agencies use a metric called cost-per-thousand (CPM) to facilitate comparisons between media. The CPM formula is:

$$CPM = (cost\ of\ media\ buy\ /\ total\ impressions) \times 1,000$$

While CPMs can be used to compare the efficiencies of different media, they rarely are used to do so. This is because the decision to use a medium is usually based on larger factors, such as whether visuals are necessary to explain the proposition clearly.

But agencies do use CPM comparisons to select specific vehicles within a media category. For example, if a company decides to use print, it will generate CPMs for the various publications under consideration and then select titles based on their efficiency.

Agencies generally use target CPMs, rather than total CPMs. A CPM based on total audience presumes that every person in that audience is a potential user. But, as previously discussed, only a certain percentage of the total audience will comprise the actual target, so we focus on just those individuals when making comparisons.

Media selections cannot be made solely on the basis of CPMs, however, because media that delivers to a highly concentrated target typically has low reach. Therefore, campaigns must include broader-reach media, which may not be as efficient in delivering the target, to ensure adequate reach. It's a delicate balancing act that is determined by increasingly sophisticated modeling techniques.

Balance efficiency with reach to create effective plans.

Seasonal Timing
Very few advertisers have the necessary resources to advertise consistently throughout the entire year. Fortunately, very few products are bought consistently throughout the year, so it is fairly simple to focus campaigns based on the product's or service's seasonality.

But an advertiser may still need to further condense efforts within seasonal parameters to achieve impact. Typically, this is done through flighting. This entails running ads for several weeks, taking a break, and then beginning again. Research indicates that while memories fade over time, placing additional weight behind the effort after only a short hiatus increases overall memory.[6] Traditionally, most advertisers use a four-week-on/three-week-off/four-week-on pattern.

The advent of modeling has introduced an alternative approach to communications planning called the recency theory. This theory, which is appropriate only for brands with flat seasonality, postulates that since the consumer is equally likely to buy the product at any time of the year, it makes sense to have a low level of communications taking place all year round to constantly remind the consumer of its existence.[7]

Tailor your efforts to the brand's seasonality.

Geography

Reducing scope is another way to increase impact with limited funding. Fewer eyeballs cost less money. Most brands have uneven sales patterns, which makes it easy to focus efforts on specific regions where sales are higher; or alternatively, those where sales are lower and there is more upside potential.

During a roll-out, one or several markets are targeted for a given period of time. After that, the effort moves to new markets. While this technique is typically used when new products are introduced and only limited quantities are available during the initial stage of the launch, it can also be used to stretch limited budgets.

Roll-outs are also used if timing will vary based on geography. Scotts' Turf Builder provides a good example. This product is designed to be used in the spring. But, spring comes earlier in Charlotte than it does in Buffalo. So, Scotts must use a spot media plan, one that delivers weight to different markets at different times, in order to be effective.

Because media companies charge a premium for spot television, once an advertiser's spot market coverage reaches 40 percent of U.S. households it becomes more efficient to advertise nationally instead of locally.

Another option for obtaining greater impact with limited money is to advertise in only the top ten television markets. These represent 29 percent of U.S. households and can therefore, get the message across fairly efficiently, assuming city dwellers are a good target for the brand.[8]

Consider local and regional plans for greater impact.

Chapter 15: Niche Communications Plan – Mobile Phone Service

The following is an example of a communications plan developed to summarize the information discussed in previous chapters.

A flowchart is included which is typical. It serves to summarize the plan and allows readers to see when the media runs and how it is sequenced. Costs have not been included, but normally these would be noted to the right of each item in the plan, as would target delivery.

MOBILE PHONE SERVICE (MPS)
BUSINESS TRAVELER NICHE COMMUNICATION PLAN

Target
The primary target is Adults 25–40, who travel frequently on business.

Consumer Insight
These individuals see themselves as "Road Warriors," ready to battle obstacles as they complete their missions.

Media Objectives
Raise awareness of MPS among the key target group, Adults 25–40: the "Road Warriors."

Media Strategies
Dominate airport terminals and train stations to effectively and efficiently reach the core target as they travel.

Provide travelers with comforts while they are traveling to improve their travel experience.

Media Tactics
Airports and train stations provide a very efficient opportunity to address business travelers. We will blanket these venues with activities for the duration of the effort.

The campaign's primary focus will be a series of kiosks called "MPS Care Centers." At these booths, travelers can test the MPS service by making short calls home for free, discuss available plans, and avail themselves of MPS's hospitality.

MPS will also provide electric outlets and wireless Internet connections beside comfortable seating, as well as complementary coffee. Both the connections and the coffee cups will be branded with the MPS message.

The campaign will use additional targeted media to support the program throughout and around the airports/train stations. These include:

- Televisions in airports/train stations
- Posters in airports/train stations
- Complementary toiletries in the bathrooms
- Coffee sleeves at various food vendors
- Local area maps
- Additional outlets and wifi connections in various locations throughout the airports/train stations
- Signage on complimentary shuttle buses
- Pamphlets, signage, and complimentary mints at rental car counters
- Outdoor advertising on travel routes leading to the airports/train stations

Publicity

The kiosks will provide a compelling focus for a wide variety of publicity. We recommend creating video news releases (VNRs) and distributing a series of press releases with abundant visuals to the press for publication online and offline.

Placement for the VNRs will include online social networking sites, such as myspace.com, and appropriate travel blogs in addition to more traditional television outlets. Teaser emails will be sent in advance of the launch to generate buzz.

Timing

To maximize resources and gain learning as we proceed, this campaign will employ a roll-out strategy.

We will cover five markets at a time. Our first five will be: Atlanta, Chicago, Dallas, Los Angeles, and New York.

Markets will receive a three-month media heavy-up, when most of the media will run, followed by limited targeted activity to provide year-long coverage.

Flowchart

MCS Communication Plan 2008	Dec	Jan	Feb	Mar	Apr	May	Jun	Jul	Aug	Sep	Oct	Nov	Dec
Publicity Teaser emails													
Press Release													
Kiosks													
Airport/ Station TV													
Airport/ Station Posters													
Coffee cup Sleeves													
Complimentary Toiletries													
Local Maps													
Outlets/Wifi													
Shuttle buses/ Rental Counters													
Outdoor													

Part III: Creative Development

Chapter 16: Positioning Statements

While there are many ways to express brand strategies, one of the most common and most useful is the positioning statement.

A positioning statement summarizes the key elements of the strategy and puts them into one long, run-on sentence. It is extremely helpful in articulating a brand's strategy and achieving thought conscious among key constituents. It is also the best format for testing, because it removes all executional elements from the equation and forces people to focus only on the proposition being expressed.

While formats vary slightly, the one below captures all essential elements.

Positioning Statement Format

To _____(target market)_____,

who _____(consumer insight)_____,

Brand XYZ _____(frame of reference)_____,

Is _____(point of difference)_____,

because _____(reasons to believe)_____.

Here is an example of a positioning statement from *Kellogg on Branding*:

To the tradesman who uses his power tools to make a living (target) and cannot afford downtime on the job (consumer insight), DeWalt professional power tools (frame of reference) are more dependable than other brands of professional power tools (point of difference) because they are engineered to the brand's historic high-quality standards and are backed by Black & Decker's extensive service network, and guarantee to repair or replace any tool within 48 hours (reasons to believe).[1]

I laughed when I first saw this statement, because it was so tortured, I was sure it had been developed and used by the marketers at DeWalt.

Note that the statement includes three reasons to believe: 1) engineered to the brand's historic high-quality standards, 2) backed by Black & Decker's extensive service network, and 3) guarantee to repair or replace any tool within 48 hours. As discussed previously, the rule of threes has been incorporated into the positioning statement to make it more persuasive and memorable.

Here is a slightly simpler example taken from *Contemporary Advertising*:

To 18-year-old males (target) who embrace excitement, adventure, and fun (consumer insight), Mountain Dew (frame of reference) is the great-tasting soft drink that exhilarates like no other (point of difference), because it is energizing, thirst-quenching, and has a unique citrus flavor (reasons to believe).[2]

It, too, follows the standard formula.

And here's one I wrote for a new communications service for the B-to-B market:

IT Professionals (target), Company X understands your need to stay connected and be informed (consumer insight), that's why we're introducing Y (frame of reference), a revolutionary breakthrough in integrated communications (point of difference)—a single network of virtually unlimited capacity that will enable high-speed online access, video applications, and multiple simultaneous telephone services so you can communicate in ways that have never been feasible before (reasons to believe).

It is interesting to note, that research indicates that we have become so accustomed to the use of the word "because" prior to the presentation of rationale for the claim preceding it, that using this argument structure makes the claim more credible regardless of the support provided.[3]

This positioning statement was one of several developed and then tested to see which one was the most salient. When we tested them, we were concerned that they had become too long, so we included options that did not provide reasons to believe, and, instead, ended after the point of difference. We discovered that statements excluding support did not test as well as complete ones, which was consistent with the academic research cited above.

Detailed arguments are more persuasive.

Chapter 17: Creative Strategies

There are, undoubtedly, an infinite number of creative strategies. As discussed previously, the best strategies are derived from knowledge of the target and insight into that target's behavior, which can often be gleaned from research.

Strategy transcends both category and medium. Back in 1993, I transferred from the L'Oreal account to the AT&T business-to-business account. Many people commented on what a big change this was, except for Doug Ritter, who remarked: "I don't see what the big deal is. We cost more and we're worth it too!" And of course, he was right; both brands were using the same premium strategy at the time.

Below are thirteen strategies, which are frequently used because of their proven effectiveness.

1. Introductory
One of the primary purposes of advertising has always been to create awareness for a new product, service, or brand. Introducing and new are both very powerful words in marketing, and there is ample evidence that they positively affect sales.

Due to this fact, these words can only be used for a limited time period. The Federal Trade Commission (FTC) mandates that both words may only be used for six months, after an appropriate product modification, to prevent consumers from being mislead. Once that timeframe has expired, communications must be altered to remove these words.[1]

2. Superiority
In many cases, companies not only want to explain what a product does, but also discuss how it is superior in accomplishing its task. Typically, non-comparative superiority claims require strong support to be believable.

Fusion Razor
The campaign for the Gillette Fusion razor provides a solid example of a superiority strategy that was significantly enhanced by its support.

The advertising claimed that this was "the best razor ever," which could easily be mistaken for puffery. But the support for the claim included three strong reasons to believe, which were well-explained in the creative:

1. It's new from Gillette—the razor category leader.
2. It has five blades on one side of the razor for a closer shave.
3. It has a single precision blade on the other side for better trimming.

Altogether, Gillette builds a compelling, and ultimately, successful story. The Fusion razor captured 55 percent of all new razor sales in the United States just four weeks after its launch.[2]

Parity claims

An interesting sub-section to superiority claims is parity claims that are disguised as superiority claims. Consider this example: "Nothing keeps you drier." If you think about the true meaning of that phrase, you will see that the advertisers are not saying "We keep you the driest." They are saying "We're all the same."

3. Price/Value

Everybody wants a good deal, so price/value strategies are popular with both marketers and buyers, especially during the current recession. At the simplest level, they involve conveying a low product cost—think dollar menus.

Suave

Another form of a price/value strategy is claiming to replicate results achieved by more expensive products but at lower out-of-pocket costs. The campaign for Suave shampoo uses this strategy effectively. Its introductory tagline said: "Suave does what theirs does, for a lot less." It certainly worked for me. I am still a loyal user many years later.

4. Health Benefit

As more and more baby boomers receive their AARP membership cards, health issues have skyrocketed to the forefront. Along with the plethora of pharmaceutical advertising, we now see consumer products making health claims backed by new research to attract newly health-conscious individuals.

Pom Juice

One of my favorite examples of this is an ad for Pom Juice. An introductory poster from 2002 featured the headline: *Cheat Death*, with a visual of the bottle with a noose around its neck. The body copy read: "The antioxidant power of pomegranate juice." Wow!

Of course, my first thought after reading the headline was: "How did they substantiate such a hard-hitting claim?" Then I read the copy and realized it was based on recently released research about the health benefits of antioxidants. And, a visit to their web site confirmed that they had actually commissioned $35 million in research on the juice itself.

I happen to love pomegranates, so I was an easy sell. But I knew this ad had struck a chord with its target when I came home one night to find Pom Juice in my refrigerator. My husband, who has never found a fruit or vegetable that he actually likes, must be feeling his own mortality since he's the one who purchased it.

And, he wasn't the only one who did. In just three years, consumption of pomegranates and their juice increased ten-fold, and Pom reported $50 million in annual sales for 2005.[3]

Note: While I have read articles about the prevalence of unsupported claims in advertising, I never made any. Nor did any of the people I worked with. All the advertising claims we used were supported by statistically significant research results that were scrutinized by both lawyers and network clearance departments before they were approved for production.

5. Comparative

Comparatives are used in a variety of ways in advertising, often in combination with other strategies, as demonstrated above by the Suave example. They are effective because they help us understand the featured product by connecting it to what we already know about other products. This is particularly helpful when introducing a brand that addresses a new niche.

Oust

The 2006 ads for Oust air deodorizer featured a comparison to

Lysol, that explained that the two brands were not the same but were synergistic. This meant consumers would not replace their Lysol with Oust, but, instead, buy both. It appears to have been a successful strategy since Lysol has since started marketing its own Lysol Air Freshener.

Comparisons can also be more specific than a non-comparative claim—for example, stating "healthier than Product X" instead of simply "healthy" can be perceived as more believable because it provides more detail. Mentioning the other product by name gets tricky though. If Product X is the category leader there is a danger that all the viewer may remember from the commercial is Product X. There is also the danger of losing sight of consumers needs and focusing instead on beating the other company. The results can be negative all around as they were when Campbell's and Progresso ran a series of ads with each accusing the other of containing MSG. They convinced me not to buy either brand.

6. Preemptive

A preemptive strategy picks an aspect of a particular product and features that trait in communications before anyone else takes a similar approach. This is a particularly interesting strategy because the differentiator discussed does not have to be exclusive to the product or make the product superior. But, once one advertiser makes the claim, it is difficult for another product to discuss that same trait unless that product is prepared to make a comparative claim.

AT&T and Sprint

When I worked on AT&T in the early 90s, one of my responsibilities was to support the product claims we made in commercials with the appropriate research results. During my three years on the business the research clearly showed that the superiority of AT&T's voice quality versus Sprint was declining rapidly. Toward the end of my tenure, the differential was so low it was clear that the claim would be unsupportable in the future. Therefore, when I began working on Sprint two years later, I suggested that they consider making a claim of superior quality. Their response? "We can't do that. AT&T owns quality."

7. Luxury

Many luxury goods advertisers attempt to convince rich and poor alike that purchasing their products will be a life-altering event that will turn the users from average people into superstars.

This strategy is particularly ironic in the face of the recent happiness studies that found people who use their money to buy experiences rather than things are generally happier. The reason is simple: Once you buy a thing, its value declines as it becomes used, while memories generally become rosier over time.[4]

After this research was published in 2006, VISA's new campaign, which used the tagline *Life Takes Visa*, focused on giving members access to exclusive events and hard-to-get-into restaurants. That having been said, the traditional approach has sold a lot of cars, jewelry, and perfume.

8. Premium

The crux of premium positioning is that the item costs a bit more but is still a good value because it is a better product.

L'Oreal

L'Oreal is a perfect example of a brand that uses a premium strategy and has done so for years. According to McCann-Erickson lore, the cosmetic company's tagline "It costs more, but I'm worth it," was developed by a female copywriter back when they were rare. She was apparently in therapy at the time, and her own exploration of self-esteem led to the development of the classic line. It is interesting to note that L'Oreal has never discussed the amount of the premium consumers pay for its products, nor tried to minimize it.

AT&T

AT&T, on the other hand, ran a campaign in 1993 that characterized the price differential between it and its inferior competitors as being "just a few cents." It was an incredibly effective strategy. Because AT&T had deep pockets, our agency was able to track consumer perceptions of the brand weekly. When we saw price perceptions, i.e. the perceived difference in cost between AT&T and its competitors, beginning to rise, we would run those commercials over the weekend, and like magic, the price perceptions would go back down the following week.

9. Guarantees

One of my former bosses loved using guarantees. What's not to love? Whenever agencies do research and they ask people if they want a guarantee, they say yes; why wouldn't they? Who doesn't want reassurance that a company stands behind its products? But, even when given an explicit guarantee, few people ever bother to exercise it. So, guarantees end up costing companies very little. Definitely a win-win strategy.

Lens Crafters

Lens Crafters has been featuring a guarantee in their advertising for the last few years. Anyone who wears prescription glasses knows that picking out new frames is a difficult task because you can't see what they look like when you try them on. That means a liberal guarantee policy is a definite plus, since you might make a mistake. But, glasses tend to be very expensive, so it seems unlikely that Lens Crafters would be able to afford the campaign if many people actually returned their glasses.

The company announced in 2008 that it was extending the campaign to China, where the cost for a good pair of glasses is roughly equal to one month's salary. It will be interesting to see if the approach works with even higher financial stakes.

10. Local Appeal

Local campaigns can be used to build awareness for products with local availability or that are specifically tailored to meet community needs. When Scotts Turf Builder introduced new formulas for southern lawns, a series of radio ads were created that mentioned the names of specific southern cities. The ads ran in their respective cities, and the message was clear: This product is good for your lawn.

Campaigns that run in limited geographical areas can also often make deeper connections with locals by using inside jokes and local celebrities. In New York City, Manhattan Mini Storage takes great joy in running jokes that are consistent with local political leanings. President Bush was one of their favorite targets. And Fresh Direct uses Spike Lee and Cynthia Nixon in its ads to demonstrate the range of New Yorkers who can benefit from its services.

Absolut

Absolut Vodka's 2008 fantasy world campaign included a billboard on Manhattan's Upper East Side that featured the much anticipated Second Avenue subway line, which is not due in real life until 2018, unless of course it is delayed again by the time you read this. It's a fantasy that probably only Upper East Side locals really care about.

11. Social causes

Advertising that involves charitable causes is growing. In surveys, 77% of shoppers say they would prefer to select a brand that supports a cause, and 49% say they will go out of their way to find it.[5] Research also indicates that women will pay an extra 6.1 percent for products associated with a social cause. This is because consumers want to do business with a company that shares their social values. It harkens back to what we have already discussed about emotions being the primary driver in purchase decisions.[6]

Pedigree

An interesting example of a successful campaign that focuses on social causes is Pedigree's animal adoption campaign. Launched in 2004, it really picked up momentum in 2008 when commercials that featured potential adoptees were so compelling the company had to create follow-up spots reassuring the public their favorites had landed new homes.

According to John Anton, director of Pedigree brand marketing, the campaign not only raised $2 million for dog shelters, but also resulted in double-digit growth for the company's dry and wet dog food lines. As a result, Pedigree ran a pool-out during the *Super Bowl* in 2009.[7]

12. Going Green

Another strategy gaining momentum is going green. Not surprisingly, many of the messages generated by advertisers eager to capitalize on the trend have given rise to great skepticism. The jury is still out on whether these messages will ultimately prove effective. Since more people talk about being green than actually demonstrate it, advertisers that want to successfully use this strategy and create a compelling argument need to dig deep into consumer insights to understand why consumers are not acting on their feelings.

Ford Escape Hybrid

One example of an advertiser who has successfully done this is Ford. In 2006, it ran a campaign for the Ford Escape Hybrid that featured Kermit the Frog telling folks that "It is easy to be green."

Using the familiar kid's character reminded parents that going green is worth extra hassle and expense because they are doing it for their children. (Great consumer insight!) Sales for the Ford Escape Hybrid went up 115 percent in March 2006.[8]

13. Corporate

This strategy is on the decline. Corporate anthem commercials, which typically run during broad-reach programs such as the *Super Bowl* and Sunday morning thought leader news shows, are perceived to be a luxury that most advertisers can no longer afford.

But some, such as Anheuser Busch, still use them to soften negative imagery that may be associated with their products.

Anheuser Busch's executions are typically feel-good, soft-sell efforts with a "drive safely" message at the end. My personal favorite from a past Olympics showed a baby Clydesdale pulling a cart with the secret aid of two adult horses pushing from behind. The feel good message behind the ad was: keep practicing and eventually you will be able to do it.

Classic creative strategies work because we are familiar with these constructs.

Chapter 18: Branding

Over the past few years branding has become a very popular buzz word. But it's really just another strategy for selling stuff. It's an approach that seeks to build preference in a more abstract way, focusing not on specific product features and claims, but instead, on more indirect motivators, such as likeability.

Its increased usage is most likely due, in part, to our increased understanding about the role emotions play in purchase decisions. Six other factors also contribute to its ascent.

1. Products → Services

When I entered the advertising business in the early 1980s, most advertising sold products, such as soaps, beverages, candy, etc. Ted Bates, one of the premier agencies of the day, actually had an on-site laboratory at its New York office that was staffed by a resident scientist. Advertisers used the lab to conduct experiments on their products to help them find hooks for campaigns, such as Ivory soap's "so pure it can float" claim.

But, by the early 1990s new categories of marketers that sold services, such as long distance phone companies, emerged. Since these companies offered a variety of plans tailored to the needs of specific target segments, and the needs of the target were not static, they had to sell consumers on the idea of using their portfolio of products rather a specific offering.

2. Product Proliferation

Life used to be simpler. Once upon a time, there was only Coke and Pepsi. Now there is Coke, Diet Coke, Coke Light, Coke Zero, and so on. I'll never forget when my parents told me they went to the store to buy soda and there were so many choices they walked out without buying anything.

The numbers of products in every category have increased. For example, according to one study, there were 1,349 cameras on the market in 2006.[1] I bet there are even more on the market today.

So, how does a consumer begin to decide which one to buy? Usually the first step is to pick a brand.

3. Lack of Differentiation

There's a classic joke in advertising, from the legendary Rosser Reeves, founder of Ted Bates and father of the USP (unique selling proposition). It goes like this: A client walks into the office. He puts two nickels down on a table. He points to the one on the right and says: "This one is mine. Sell it." While differentiating between similar products is not a new problem, it is even tougher these days due to the aforementioned product proliferation.

Dell

Let's assume you have two products that are essentially the same—in this case, computers. They have the same amount of memory, use the same chips, and cost roughly the same price. How do you decide which one to buy? If it was 2001, you would have chosen the Dell, because it was recommended by an expert—Steven. Steven was a character created to advertise Dell computers and he was the quintessential expert of his day. He was a teen computer nerd who knew everything about computers during a time when most people were struggling to catch up.

This campaign is particularly interesting because Steven was designed to appeal to members of the tech community. He was one of them. They embraced him as their own, and made Dell their computer brand of choice. Therefore, when people asked techies for their recommendations, they said buy a Dell. And, for those of us paying $100 an hour for tech support, that recommendation carried considerable weight. My first three computers were all Dells, thanks to Steven.

Unfortunately, as often happens, the company ran out of ideas for using Steven and walked away from him. With his departure, Dell's brand personality became murky, and the preference for Dell among techies declined. By 2008, the brand was no longer the top seller. And, my newest computer is an HP.

4. Consumer → B-to-B

Most advertising is still consumer focused. But, business-to-business advertising has increased significantly in the past few decades. This is due to new media options that deliver more targeted audiences. The business community can now be reached very efficiently via Sunday morning news programming on the networks, CNN, *The Wall Street Journal,* and forbes.com, along with numerous similar outlets.

These campaigns are often designed to appeal to the broader business community in addition to potential clients, since many of the ads are for publicly traded companies that want to influence current stockholders, potential stockholders, and politicians too.

GE Ecoimagination

This campaign was designed to raise awareness about the green products in General Electric's portfolio. My favorite spot featured an elephant dancing in the rain to the song with the same title. It was whimsy at its finest. And it was successful. Between 2005 and 2007, sales for this division of the company doubled to reach more than $12 billion dollars.[2]

5. Value of Brand Equity

What exactly is the value of brand equity? Most people agree that it translates into an ability to sell a product at a premium price. But, it can have other less measurable advantages as well, such as acting as a barrier to entry for potential competitors and allowing more time to react to a competitive threat.[3] According to Interbrand, the brand with the highest brand equity is Coca-Cola, and the value of that equity is $67 billion.[4]

6. Globalization

A growing number of companies are now multinational, and many people work and visit countries in which they were not born. So, advertisers need to manage their brands on a global basis. My first multinational account was French-owned L'Oreal, in 1992; and in 1996, I was part of the team at McCann-Erickson that launched Lucent Technologies globally.

Diet Coke

Here are two photographs of me on vacation. What am I drinking? (Hint: Both cans are white with red type.)

© Edward Lindquist 1989, 2000

If you answered, Diet Coke, or more accurately Coke Light as it is called overseas, you are correct. I do not speak Hebrew, the language on the left, or Arabic, the language on the right, but like you, I recognized the branding for the product and therefore was able to buy Diet Coke even though I am not multilingual.

Lucent Technologies
In 1996, when Lucent Technologies was launched globally, it was the largest initial public offering (IPO) ever. And, it provided a rare opportunity to build a brand personality from scratch. McCann-Erickson was invited, along with AT&T's other roster agencies, to compete for the business of "The New Company"—a spin-off created by joining the equipment divisions of AT&T and Bell Labs.

The creative team traveled to Bell Labs to meet with some of the company's key researchers. Joyce King Thomas and Jeroen Bours returned with the inspired notion that the people who worked at this company were the type of people who were "so brilliant they forgot to put their socks on in the morning." How very Einstein.

Then, they took the notion to the next level and asked themselves, "If these people did their own advertising, what would it look like?" A few key themes emerged—an awkwardness to the copy, stripped down visuals, and a retail orientation.

"The voice" was developed to represent the theoretical Lucent employee. A stream-of-consciousness approach was used in the copy, which included modest recollections of phenomenal achievements, such as "invented dial tone" and "Have won awards (Nobel, etc.)" The concept was engaging and charming in its naiveté. The latter phrase resonated most with the audience, and many people played it back to me after the campaign broke.

In addition to developing a global brand personality, we needed to explain what the company actually did. The unusually long tagline used in the launch—"We make the things that make communications work"—was initially a line in the IPO presentation. But, when Carly Fiorina began sharing the presentation, she discovered it did an excellent job communicating the company's mission, so it was adapted for the campaign.

Finally, to convey the eagerness of a start-up, business cards were used as a sign-off.

Since we knew from the start this would be a global launch, it was essential for the brand personality to work on a multinational, multi-cultural basis. To accomplish this, we took great pains explaining the idea's evolution to our overseas offices and working with them to localize the campaign without losing its essence.

Since part of what made this campaign unique was the unusual juxtaposition of idioms, we avoided literal translations and focused on conveying meaning. For instance, when we wanted to run the headline "Ideas, Ideas, Ideas, Get 'em while they're hot," in Mexico, I spoke to the McCann manager in Mexico City and we worked together to arrive at a solution. Ultimately the breakthrough came when I said to him: "When you walk past a store and the retailer wants you to come in, what does he say?" I managed to catch "rapido," which means fast, and figured we got the result we wanted.

The campaign was a huge success. By October 2007, brand awareness zoomed to 91 percent in the financial sector and 80 percent among large customers. Sales in 1996 rose to $24 billion, and the stock price rose by 226 percent. [5]

Branding is just another strategy, which is employed when advertisers perceive it to be the best way to achieve success.

Chapter 19: The Creative Brief

The creative process starts with the creative brief. The creative brief serves two purposes. The first is to get all constituents on the same strategic page; the second is to inform the creative team—usually a copywriter who is an expert with words and an art director who handles the visuals—about the strategy. This team develops the final creative products based on the brief and related discussions.

The creative brief is the blueprint for the creative. It is a highly collaborative effort, and the better the brief, the better the advertising. For most of the people involved in advertising development, this is their best opportunity to positively impact the quality of the advertising.

The strategic planning department usually writes the brief. Responsibility used to lie with the account management department, but shifted to strategic planning in the 1990s when advertising strategy started focusing more on the target and less on the product.

Of course, there are exceptions. For example, when I worked on the Lucent Technologies campaign, which was a business-to-business account, I retained responsibility for the creative briefs because of the highly technical nature of the services being advertised.

The following creative brief format is based on those used at various agencies. While other clients and agencies may use slightly different versions, this format contains all the information necessary to develop successful creative, and perhaps more importantly, does not contain room for ambiguity. Because, the most important factors in creating effective briefs are clarity and focus.

The brief contains six elements that are critical for creative development. They are: target, consumer insight, key message, and three support points. The other elements provide the context for the project: objectives, geography, timing, tonality, etc. Together, all the pieces provide the direction necessary to develop advertising.

In a perfect world, a creative brief would be one page. But, the amount of required information that needs to be included usually pushes it to two pages. If a brief is longer than two pages, it will most likely contain contradictions, which will become extremely problematic when trying to develop creative. When this happens the brief fails to provide clear agreed to direction and can lead to the development of creative that does not meet expectations. So it is critical that the brief truly does reflect agreement.

Let's walk through the format together.

Creative Development Brief

Campaign name

Date

Background
(What is the purpose of the project?)

Remember, the primary purpose of this document is to brief a creative team, so include only the information they will need to know to develop the creative. Err on the side of brevity. The briefing will be presented in person, so creatives will have an opportunity to ask questions if they are unclear about something.

Communications objectives
(What do we expect to accomplish? How do we intend to measure results?)

As discussed in Chapter 13, this is a statement of the goals for the campaign. The goal often involves a communications measure, such as increase awareness by 10%. But increasingly, this somewhat soft objective has been replaced by hard sales quotas, e.g. increase sales by 15,000 units.

Creative elements
(What types of materials are being produced? tv, radio, etc.)

This is a list of the media to be used in the campaign so the creative team will understand what it needs to provide. Include lengths of the television spots (e.g., 30 seconds) and sizes and specs of print ads (e.g., full-page, 4-color), and any other relevant information. Typically, one format is used to present several ideas during the development stage. Once a direction is agreed upon the additional creative elements are developed.

Geography
(Where is the product/service currently available?)

Global, national, local, etc.

Timing
(When is the campaign scheduled to run?)

Seasonal, holiday, etc.

Target
(Who are we trying to reach? age, income, marital status, etc.)

As discussed in Chapters two and three, the brief should include, at a minimum, gender, age range, and one additional descriptor. But, more is better, and the better you understand your target and can convey that information to your creative team, the more effective they will be.

Consumer insight
(What do we know about the way our target thinks or feels that can be used to create an emotional connection with them?)

This is the element that transforms good advertising into great advertising. Spend the time necessary to go beyond the obvious and the payoff will be worth it.

Key message
(What is the <u>single</u> thought we intend to communicate?)

Be as focused and clear as possible. The more complex the thought becomes, the more difficult it is to communicate.

Support
(What are the three reasons to believe the key message?)

Use the Rule of Threes to create a compelling argument. Start with your strongest point. Remember that being specific increases believability.

Tonality
(Is the ad introductory? What type of mood are we trying to achieve?)

If this is a new product, we will definitely want to address that in the creative.

The following is a creative brief that I reverse engineered from the Disney commercial *Too Excited to Sleep*, which was discussed in Chapter 4. The commercial urged families to make a repeat visit, and used the insight that many of us have difficulty sleeping when we are excited, to illustrate that the entire family is looking forward to their impending trip to Disneyworld

Example 1: Disneyworld

Creative Development Brief
Campaign name: Disneyworld
Date: 1/06

Background
(What is the purpose of the project?)

We are seeking to drive traffic to Disneyworld during the "off season."

Communications objectives
(What do we expect to accomplish? How do we intend to measure results?)

We want to increase traffic to Disneyworld by ten percent during first quarter of 2006*. The campaign will be measured by increased reservations through the dedicated phone number, 407-W-Disney.

Creative elements
(What types of materials are being produced? Tv? Radio? Etc.)

We will use a 30-second television execution to achieve our goals.

Geography
(Where is product/service currently available?)

This is a national campaign.

Timing
(When is the campaign scheduled to run?)

The campaign will run throughout first quarter of 2006.

Target
(Who are we trying to reach? Age, income, marital status, etc.)
Our target is married Adults 25–49, with children under 12.

Consumer insight
(What do we know about the way our target thinks or feels that can be used to create an emotional connection with them?)

When people get excited they often have trouble sleeping.

Key message
(What is the single thought we intend to communicate?)

It's a good time to visit Disneyworld again.

Support
(What are three reasons to believe the key message?)

1. A family of four can take a 6-night/7-day trip to Disney World for less than $1,500, including ride tickets.
2. New rides and activities are being added all the time.
3. Disneyworld is fun for the entire family.

Tonality
(Is the ad introductory? What type of mood are we trying to achieve?)

The tonality is friendly and fun. The effort is targeted to repeat visitors.

Mandatories
(What are the executional elements that must be included?)

The dedicated reservations phone number: 407-W-Disney must be included.

Please note that I made up the communications objective because I have not read anywhere what their goals were for the campaign.

Below is another example that focuses only on the key elements. It is reverse engineered from an existing Fresh Direct commercial that features Spike Lee as a "wanna be" chef, with no cooking experience.

Example 2: Fresh Direct

Creative Development Brief
Campaign name: Fresh Direct – one-click recipes introduction
Date: October 2006

<u>Target</u>
(Who are we trying to reach? age, income, marital status, etc.)

The target is Adults 25–45, who live in New York City, and are responsible for their own meals.

Consumer insight

(What do we know about the way our target thinks or feels that can be used to make an emotional connection with them?)

They can't cook, but they'd like to.

Key message

(What is the single thought we intend to communicate?)

With new one-click recipes from Fresh Direct, anyone can cook great dinners.

Support

(What are the three reasons to believe the key message?)

1. There are hundreds of recipes from world-class chefs on the Fresh Direct Web site.

2. You can order all the ingredients for the recipe you choose with just one mouse click.

3. Everything is delivered to your door.

Chapter 20: Creative Brief Example – Asphalt Green

Below is an original creative brief developed using information from the company's website, which is consistent with how a typical brief would be created. Sometimes clients provide specific briefings as well. Note that I have focused on one specific target segment in order to be able to provide a more persuasive message.

Creative Development Brief

Campaign Name: Asphalt Green Summer Camp
Date: 1/09

Background
(What is the purpose of the project? What are the defined parameters?)

Asphalt Green is a non-profit health club dedicated to assisting individuals of all ages and backgrounds to achieve health through a lifetime of sports and fitness.

While it serves multiple audiences in the community with customized programs, its offerings for children are particularly robust encompassing both aquatic and non-aquatic options.

The purpose of this campaign is increase enrollment in the summer camp.

Communications Objectives
(What do we expect to accomplish? How do we intend to measure results?)

We expect to increase enrollment over previous year by 10 percent. Results will be measured by tracking sign-ups.

Creative Elements
(What types of materials are being produced? TV? Radio? Etc.)

- School Posters
- Local websites and mommy blogs.

Geography
(Where is service currently available? Where will it expand within the next 12 months?)

Asphalt Green is located on Manhattan's Upper East Side, at 91st Street and York Avenue.

Timing
(When is the campaign scheduled to run?)

The campaign will run in April and May 2009.

Target

(Who are we trying to reach? age, income, marital status, etc.)

The target is Women 18–49, with kids ages 4–14, and household incomes of $50K+.

Consumer Insight

(What do we know about the way our target thinks or feels that can be used to make an emotional connection with them?)

Moms are always looking to place their children in stimulating environments, so the kids can grow as individuals.

Key Message

(What is the single thought we intend to communicate?)

Asphalt Green is the perfect summer camp for your kids, because it gives them a chance to experience and learn new things.

Support

(What are the reasons to believe the key message?)

1. Asphalt Green's personalized instructions make it easy for children to learn a new sport or perfect an old one.

2. Participation in team sports will enhance kids' skills and teach them how to get along with others.

3. To further exercise the mind, in addition to sports, Asphalt Green's summer programs include cultural activities, such as museum visits.

Tonality
(Is the ad introductory? Is it focused on acquisition or retention, etc?)

In keeping with the spirit of the club, the tonality of the creative should be upbeat and fun.

Mandatories
(What are the executional elements that must be included?)

We want to include the Web site address: www.asphaltgreen.org; the email address: camps@asphaltgreen.org; and a dedicated phone number: 212-369-8890, x104, in all communications.

Chapter 21: Creative Development

A student once asked me if I was going to teach him how to create ads. It was an interesting question, and I gave it some thought. But, the truth is that much as we would like to turn the creative process into a science, it is, in fact, an art. And you can't teach people how to create advertisements anymore than you can teach them how to draw a picture or shoot a movie.

However, you can inspire creativity. Most of the creative people I know and respect are great consumers of media. They tend to have stacks of magazines on their floors and attend cutting edge film festivals. In short, they study their craft.

They also work very hard. They put in long hours, and I can't imagine what the pressure is like to be creative on deadline. They are professionals, and deserve respect for their expertise from clients.

Therefore, it baffles me that marketing personnel who have undergraduate business degrees and MBAs, but have never taken a creative writing course in their lives, think they can write better than someone who was trained in the subject. And yet, so many do.

I can still recall one incident with a client product manager. We had spent weeks working on a very copy-heavy, multi-page insert. One evening, around 7:30 p.m. she said to me: "I can write better copy than this." That was the last straw. I wished her luck, hung up the phone, and left for the evening. The next morning she called back. And, without even apologizing, launched into a long list of revisions she needed, including the ones she had asked for the previous evening and hadn't done herself. So it wasn't so simple after all.

Similarly, an art direction-related incident haunts me. A client with business degrees but no art classes to his credit, requested that the final shot of the product in the commercial make as much of an impact as possible. We provided a product shot that was cropped so the product's edges were cut off. This gave the illusion that the product too big to be contained within the television screen. When he saw it, he said: "No. I want it straight-forward, dead center." Needless to say, this option did not create as much of an impact.

The biggest mistake clients make is getting too specific with their feedback, rather than just articulating their general concerns. We once created a print ad where the visual, which was a passport with stamps, lacked excitement. The client attempted to fix this by giving very specific art direction, telling us which stamps to darken, and which to lighten. But, because she lacked the artistic knowledge necessary to really know how to fix the problem her direction was counter-productive. In fact, it accentuated the problem.

Luckily, I was able to read between the lines. So, when I spoke to the art director, I asked him to create two versions—one that addressed the client's direction and one where he would "make the visual more exciting." When the client saw the two options side-by-side, she realized the agency version was, in fact, the correct solution for the problem.

Clients need to respect their creatives' expertise. If they don't, they should get new ones.

Chapter 22: Executional Formats

Just as certain strategies appear frequently in advertising, many formats for executing—or conveying—the creative message are also used frequently because of their proven effectiveness.

Below are descriptions of twelve commonly used executional formats.

1. Unknown Stand-up Presenters

Having someone speak directly to an audience is the most basic form of communication, and is a direct translation of what typically happens in one-to-one sales. When an unknown presenter is used in a television commercial, then the effectiveness of the advertising relies heavily upon the strength of the talent selected.

2. Celebrity Endorsements

A variation of the unknown stand-up presenter is using a known presenter, such as a celebrity. I am not a fan of using celebrities. While it is true that they attract attention, it is unclear whether this translates into sales increases that are significant enough to justify their salary. And sometimes their presence can be so distracting that it inhibits communication of the message. Or they hawk so many different products that their credibility comes into question.

Sometimes a celebrity is used as a voice-over rather than on-camera talent. Usually the justification is that the celebrity is a better actor than regular voice-over talent and can better communicate the message. Many times, I am hard pressed to recognize a celebrity voice-over. But, some people are better at this than I am, so the significance of the person selected can matter.

AT&T

In the early 1990s AT&T used Dick Cavett as a voice-over for its B-to-B commercials. I can still remember listening to a woman in a focus group saying "You use Dick Cavett for your voice-over and he's really smart."

3. Authority Figures

Presenters can also be authority figures. The classic example is someone in a white coat presenting scientific information. Actors playing both doctors and pharmacists often appear in drug advertising, to reassure consumers the information being conveyed is scientifically accurate. It's ironic, since they themselves are not legitimate doctors or pharmacists. Years ago, someone did a funny twist on this by using an actor who portrayed a doctor on a soap opera as a presenter. He began the spot by saying "I'm not a doctor, but I play one on TV…"

4. User Testimonials

Advertisers also use real people in testimonials. They do this because they assume that audiences are jaded, and recognize that advertising messages are typically delivered by paid spokespeople. It is presumed therefore that people will find real users more credible.

This drives word-of-mouth marketing in general and blogs in particular. As Malcolm Gladwell points out in *The Tipping Point*, there are people among us who have expert knowledge in certain areas and it is not uncommon to seek opinions from them before making decisions. The mommy blogs, in particular, are becoming increasingly powerful as other women seek their advice and counsel, and these days major companies are seeking to create tighter bonds with them to elicit their support.

5. Vignettes

People learn by listening to stories. That's why we dream. The new information that we have learned that day is strung together with things we already know in a story format, which helps us to create the links necessary to put the new information into long term memory.[1] The three-part structure used in the vignette format—set-up, problem, and resolution — allows consumers to clearly understand what the product does and what need it can fulfill. And, of course, it ties into the *Rule of Threes*.

Storytelling can also focus on an emotional presentation instead of a straight-forward one, which can help advertisers achieve the emotional connection they want to make with the audience.

American Airlines

A 2006 commercial for American Airlines featured a businessman who carried a lot of guilt about leaving his daughter behind as he left for a never-ending stream of international business trips. While he kept in touch via phone, the payoff came at the end of the trip when he used his frequent flier miles to take her with him. It's a familiar scenario; my husband and I went to the Caribbean.

6. Metaphors

Metaphors can communicate complex ideas, add creativity, and increase emotional response. They are typically used when the goal is to sell a portfolio of products or a broader relationship with the company.

AT&T Rollercoaster

In one B-to-B television commercial, AT&T used a rollercoaster as a metaphor for the ups and downs of business. It was an effective way to connect with the audience and to demonstrate that AT&T understood the challenges that they faced.

7. Montage

A montage features a series of visuals edited together. Because the cost of shooting increases with the number of sets/locations and the amount of talent used, montages can be expensive to create, and therefore, are used less often.

The exception is when footage already exists, so the only cost involved is editing. Movie advertising is a good example. Depending how the existing film is edited, the movie can take on an entirely different color. How often have you seen a hilarious trailer, only to find that when you saw the movie, all the best jokes were in the trailer?

8. Copy Only

In the early days of advertising, ads were copy heavy and provided a lot of information. Today, consumers prefer shorter, more succinct ads. However, pithy copy can still successfully attract attention and make a point.

Prevage

A few years ago, Prevage was introduced using outdoor with a headline that read: "Make your birth date look like a misprint." It blew me away. That's one heck of a promise for anyone over a certain age, and shows a keen understanding of the target. So it's not surprising that they responded.

According to *The New York Times,* 300,000 bottles of the prescription-only product were sold in just three months.[2]

9. Animation

The use of animation in commercials is growing and will continue to do so because of economics. The cost of producing live-action commercials continues to increase, while the cost of developing animation is decreasing, making the latter more appealing. Animation also allows advertisers to create images they can't do with only live action, which often helps them achieve both greater breakthrough and better communication.

California Cheese

A good example of effective animation is the series of talking cow commercials for California cheese. The engaging nature of these spots, which feature talking cows with a wry sense of humor, draw the audience in, while effectively communicating the idea that cows raised in such a idyllic environment must produce better cheese.

The spots, which originally ran only in California, were so successful that the campaign was expanded nationally. And, in spring 2007, California surpassed Wisconsin as the number one cheese-producing state in the United States.[3]

10. Voice-Over

Most commercials use a combination of on-camera talent and voice-over. The former is used to make an emotional connection with the audience, while the latter is used to deliver technical information.

Sometimes, however, advertisers opt to use all voice-over. The separation of the words from the visual allows for a greater number of visuals, since people can absorb visuals much faster than they can words.[4] As a result, storytelling can be greatly enhanced.

Suave

A good example of this is a commercial for Suave shampoo that ran in 2008. It featured a mom who appeared to be unconcerned with her unglamorous appearance, and included an overt reference to the consumer insight: "89 percent of moms admit they let themselves go." The ad told this particular mom's life story through a series of quick edit-cuts, starting with her engagement and continuing through her present status as a mother with a dog, two kids, and another on the way. As the story progresses, it becomes clear why her priorities have changed.

11. Demonstrations

Advertisers use demonstrations in a variety of ways. Demonstrations can clarify what the product does, provide reasons to believe in its efficacy, and show superiority over competitors through side-by-side, split-screen comparisons.

L'Oreal
Many L'Oreal ads include a product demonstration that highlights the scientific underpinning of the product. The rationale is that including technical information helps support the basic product proposition that L'Oreal products are superior because they are backed by better research.

12. Music
Initially commercials used custom music, including tailored jingles, almost exclusively. Many of these are true classics, such as ones written by Barry Manilow during his pre-*Mandy* days. Who can forget: "You deserve a break today?"

Once it became more acceptable for popular musicians to use their music for commercial purposes, we started hearing familiar tunes, sometimes even performed by the original artists. These songs have the distinct advantage of evoking a memory, which enables the advertising to make an immediate emotional connection with the audience.

Target
The first time my husband saw the Target commercial that uses the Beatle's song *Hello, Goodbye*, he was horrified to see the logo for Lysol displayed. But, once I explained to him that Target was actually a pretty cool company he was somewhat mollified.

These days, original music for commercials is making a comeback. But this time the music is being written by artists who already have a following. And, merchandising of the songs becomes part of the campaign, often through free downloads or premium CDs.

<u>Chevy</u>

Chevy was the first company to have a major breakthrough with this idea, in 2008, when John Mellencamp's *My Country* was introduced as the new Chevrolet theme. It became so popular through this commercial that when it was released as a single, it shot to the top of the charts.

Chapter 23: The Production Process

Maximizing campaign quality is always the main goal for everyone involved in creating advertising. Clients can help achieve this goal by both contributing to the development of a focused creative brief and giving the creative team enough time to develop quality concepts.

Allowing creatives adequate time may sound odd when many clients only produce a single commercial every one to two years. But, work does expand to fill the time allotted, and often, brief development takes longer than expected, leaving the creative team with inadequate time to develop its concepts.

Allow two full weeks for creative development.

Two weeks is the sweet spot for creative development. Any less time, and the ideas may disappoint; any more time and the team gets distracted by other assignments.

Time is also important to the production process. Typically, print and television ads are created using ad hoc teams. Freelance experts are hired to help, based on the particular needs of the assignment. When given sufficient time to plan ahead, they select the partners who can most effectively and efficiently complete the jobs. But, when the start of production is delayed, and it becomes necessary to complete the task in a shortened timeframe producers may have to use new freelancers, and the resulting learning curve slows the process.

Rush jobs also require additional supervision from account staff and producers, because employees have to produce the creative in a timeframe they are not comfortable with. Clients need to provide extra cooperation as well.

The following pages provide examples of timelines and the processes used to create print and television ads in standard time frames.

Print Production Timeline

The graphic below outlines a print production timeline, followed by a description of each element and the time allotted for completion.

Print Production Process

2 weeks for search 3 weeks for prep	1 week	2 weeks	3 weeks	1 week

Stock Search

Review stock
Select photo

Or

Photographer Search

Bid/Award job

Prep shoot

location/
set design
props
casting
wardrobe

Shoot

Select Photo

Mechanical Develop-ment

Retouching

Compositing
Color Correction
Effects

Proofing

Review/
Corrections
3 rounds

Materials

Ship
2 1/2 mo.
for
magazines

© PJ Lehrer 2009

The entire process for producing printed materials takes approximately twelve weeks. More complex executions that contain multiple visuals, heavy special effects, and overseas locations will require additional time.

1. Stock visual/photographer search: two weeks

Since "renting" an image is less expensive than shooting an original piece of art, the production process begins with a stock photography search. As of press time, Getty Images was the stock photography market leader. The company offers a variety of images in a broad price range, based on how widely the image will be seen (impressions) and how long it will be used (timing). While I have used stock photography for collateral materials, such as brochures, I never found the exact image we wanted for an ad and always had to shoot an original visual.

If you plan to shoot an original image, the next step is to search for a photographer. Photographer searches are guided by art buyers, who are experts on still photographers and familiar with a variety of artists with different specialties. Based on a discussion with the creative team about the goals for the visual, the art buyer will ask to see portfolios of photographers that might be suitable for the job. He will review the look books with the creative team and they will make a joint recommendation.

Because the out-of-pocket cost for print production is relatively low (approximately $50,000 for a one-page, four-color ad), seeking specifications and pricing from three photographers, a process known as triple-bidding, is usually not necessary. Instead, only a recommendation and back-up are selected. Following selection, the person in charge of print traffic puts together a cost estimate and timeline for the job and it is awarded.

2. Pre-production: three weeks

The first step in setting up a shoot is to decide whether the shot will be taken on a set or on location. Advantages of using a set include plentiful electricity, complete customization of surroundings, and minimal crew transport. When shooting on location, photographers often have to bring in additional electricity, and logistics can get complicated and expensive. However, if the shoot requires a large set, going on location is often more cost effective than building a set.

Remember that everything that appears in the shot is intentional; nothing is there by accident. So, a team of people is needed to decide everything from the type of plate that rice will be placed on (if the ad is for a rice product) to who does the placing. A variety of specialists handle these decisions, including location scouts, casting agents, stylists, and wardrobe experts.

Viewers will notice even the most subtle of these details. In the past, I have fielded phone calls from individuals who wanted to know where they could get the lamp in the back of the room, or the shirt the actor was wearing.

Once complete, all pre-production details are discussed in a pre-production meeting. Since all decisions are finalized at this meeting, it is widely attended, both in person and via conference call. After the meeting, senior staff usually steps aside and allows the remaining team members to oversee the shoot. Therefore, it is imperative that everything agreed to during the meeting be implemented without change.

3. Shoot: one week

If you are shooting one visual with a fairly simple set-up, the shoot may take a single day. More complicated shoots will take longer. Usually, both client and agency staff attend shoots to ensure that agreements reached during the pre-production meeting are properly implemented.

It is also important to make sure legal issues are properly addressed. For instance, there are several restrictions when working with food: Adding ingredients to a product that are not already part of it is prohibited. So, when we were shooting a rice and vegetable product, we could not replace the dried vegetables in the product with fresh ones. Nor could we add extra dried vegetables. But, we could make sure that the scoop of rice we used was one that randomly contained more vegetables, and we could arrange them so that they were more visible to the eye.

4. Photo selection/mechanical development: two weeks

While some professional photographers have switched to digital photography, others feel film provides superior quality and is worth the additional time and expense. Regardless of whether they use a digital or film camera, photographers take numerous shots of the subject, since film is cheap compared to the expense involved in redoing the shoot. The art director will review the pictures and select a "hero" shot that will be used in the advertising.

While the visual is being reviewed and selected, a mechanical is created. This is the literal blueprint for the ad. It shows each element in the ad—headline, copy, logos, visuals, etc.—in place, in the correct typefaces and size proportions, so the layout can be approved.

5. Retouching/proofing: three weeks

Once the "hero" shot has been selected, it will most likely need additional retouching to please the discerning eyes of the art director and print production person. Sometimes multiple visuals are combined —known as compositing—and on occasion additional graphics are added. These tasks, along with whatever else is needed to achieve the final visual effect is done at this stage.

Once they are complete, the mechanical and photograph are married, and the proofing process begins.

The process for four-color print production begins by separating the image into four plates: red (magenta), yellow, blue (cyan), and black. Next, the separations are run together on a press to produce the combined image. Often, slight variations in the result require that color adjustments be made to one or more of the plates. Once this is done, another proof is run. Typically, all adjustments can be made with three rounds of proofing.

6. Materials: one week

Next, materials are created for the publications. These consist of the color plates and the final proof. Since publications vary in size, slight adjustments to each ad will be made to accommodate them.

7. Shipping: two and one half months

Finally, the materials are shipped to publications for placement. Shipping lead time is typically two-and-one-half months (about 75 days) in advance of the publication date, which means the entire creative production process needs to be started five-and-one-half months before the ads will run. These long lead times are an issue for advertisers, and magazines have been striving to shorten them for years. Surprisingly, digital advances have had little impact on the overall time frame.

Television Production Timeline

Below is a sample television production timeline. It shows each element and the time allotted to complete it.

Television Production Process

3 - 4 weeks	3 - 4 weeks	1 week	3 weeks to Rough cut 1 week to finish

Director's Search

Review reels
Select 3 directors

Post - Production

Editing
Special Effects
Scratch track

Pre- Production

Bid Job

Location/set

Shoot
&
Special
Effects

Review specs
with directors

Set design
Props

Approve Rough cut

Record voice over
Add supers
Final mix

Casting
Wardrobe

Shooting Board

Award job

Dub & Ship

Approve elements in
Pre-pro meeting

Review bids
Select Director

Network: 1 week
Syndication: 2 weeks

© PJ Lehrer 2009

The basic process for producing television commercials is similar to that of print production, and takes between eleven and thirteen weeks for a simple execution.

More complex executions may involve multiple weeks of shooting and special effects, which can expand the timeline dramatically.

1. Director's search: three to four weeks

The television production process could be started with a stock footage search, like it is with print, but this is even less likely to yield viable results. So, the first step is for the creative team to meet with an agency producer to discuss their vision for the spot and which directors might be appropriate for the task. Reels for potential directors are acquired and reviewed, and three directors are selected for bidding.

Triple bidding is a critical part of the television production process, not only for cost control, but also because of the highly collaborative nature of TV production. The creative team often has an idea about how they want the ad to work, but aren't quite sure how to achieve the results they are looking for. The agency producer can help since he has more experience in that area; so can the directors, but they often have very different ideas about how to turn the vision into reality. So, the bidding process also becomes an opportunity to vet the directors and find out what they can bring to the party, based on their experience and expertise.

In the end, the lowest bid doesn't always win. Television production costs are driven to a great degree by how many set-ups the spot requires, which directly impacts how many shooting days need to be scheduled.

Since equipment and personnel are rented for the day, the difference in cost between an eight-hour day and a 12-hour day is often less than the cost of scheduling an extra half-day, even with a reduced crew. So, decisions are made based on which option will yield the best results.

2. Pre-production: three to four weeks

As with print shoots, the details for a commercial are ironed out during the pre-production process, and final approval is granted during the pre-production meeting. However, since the average cost of a television production exceeds $360,000, the financial stakes are quite a bit higher.

Among the key elements of the process is casting. As discussed previously, casting can make or break a shoot. And while it's easy to see why that's true, other seemingly less important elements, such as selecting a hair stylist for the on-camera talent, can also be critical. I once worked on a hair care account where the client insisted on using a certain stylist, despite the fact that the stylist had no expertise in styling hair for film. His lack of knowledge resulted in the model's hair appearing overly dry on camera, and ultimately a re-shoot was deemed necessary, at the agency's expense.

Typically television commercials are presented using a storyboard format. These are drawings of roughly 12–15 frames from the execution that depict the basic visuals of the spot. Underneath each visual is the copy that will be spoken as the visuals appear.

When the ad is ready for production, the director and his team use the storyboard to create a more detailed shooting board, which is shared in the pre-production meeting. It shows each frame that will be shot including camera angles and movement. This is necessary because sometimes the same set-up will be shot from several different angles, or with specialty cameras, and then the resulting footage options will be edited together in post-production.

3. Shoot: one week

Shooting time varies widely depending on the complexity of the commercial. The simplest presenter spots can take one to two days, while complicated metaphors can take several weeks. The primary objective of the shoot is to adhere to all the agreements reached during the pre-production process, and deliver the footage necessary to complete the execution as agreed. This is not as easy as it sounds.

One team arrived at the shooting location to find what they considered a lucky-strike extra—a local carnival—and were so taken with the possibilities that they tossed the agreed to parameters aside and went with the carnival. Big mistake. The senior clients, who did not attend the shoot, were expecting to see what had been agreed to at the pre-production meeting, but the agency was not able to supply it. The fact that the onsite client approved the changes was deemed irrelevant, and the agency was blamed for the mishap.

The best way to handle on-site inspirations is to make sure they don't take precedence over doing the job you were sent to do. If there's time left over, after the specs of the job have been met, then it's okay to get creative. But, if you do it before, you run the risk of ruining a relationship and possibly having to re-shoot the entire thing.

In another case, the creatives decided to wrap up before they took the money shot, which is the final shot in the commercial—the one that closes the loop on the sales proposition. When I pointed out that they had neglected to do what one might consider the most important shot in the commercial, they said they had no choice but to wrap because they had lost the light. I insisted they complete the shot before wrapping and they did; through the miracles of post-production the lighting turned out fine.

Deliver the storyboard.

Like with other forms of video production, commercials are shot out of sequence and all the scenes that use one specific location or set are shot together regardless of when they take place in the chronology of the story. On average, setting up a shot takes from one to two hours; more if the shot involves something dangerous like high speed cars or fire. During that time, lighting is adjusted, tracks are created for the camera to run on, and sound is tested. Once that set-up is ready, all scenes that take place in it are shot.

Overseas shoots

In the United States, both film crew and actors are unionized. The unions have rules about how many hours people can work per day, how often food must be served, and the length of turnover time between days. In addition, U.S. actors receive not only session fees, for the days they are actually filmed, but also talent payments based on how often the commercial runs and how many people will see it. If a commercial uses a significant amount of talent, such as crowd scenes, and the advertiser runs a fairly heavy schedule, such as telecom companies do, then quarterly talent fees can easily exceed a quarter of a million dollars. At this point, agencies begin to consider shooting overseas.

Decisions to shoot overseas are made prior to starting the director search, so that these needs may be taken into consideration when selecting a director. As more high-budget shooting moves overseas, some directors have opened secondary offices in other countries.

Some countries aren't unionized, and others allow for complete buy-outs of talent for a reasonable one-time fee, so shooting overseas can present significant savings. The agency also needs to consider current foreign exchange rates, since the relative strength or weakness of the dollar may also factor into the financials of the decision.

On the flip side, depending where the shoot takes place, creative issues can emerge. If the commercial requires talent to speak on camera, then language barriers can become a problem. And, even if the people in the commercial don't speak, there can be diversity issues with casting in other countries. Communicating with different time zones is less of a problem than it was pre-Internet, but issues still come up from time to time.

Special effects

The use of animation combined with live action shots has increased as the technology has improved and costs have come down. Sometimes, the special effects are so critical to the overall effectiveness of the creative, and their cost is so high, that they too are triple bid. In these cases, it is likely the development of the effects will also take longer and will need to be started earlier in the process in order to complete the commercial on time.

4. Post-production: three to four weeks

The first stage of the post-production process involves selecting the best takes and editing them together. Since there are usually at least a dozen takes per scene, it's a time consuming process. A scratch track is added using borrowed music to give viewers an idea of the type of music to be used, and the copywriter usually records all the copy in a voice-over. The result is called the "rough cut."

Next, all the constituents including the clients review the rough cut. Sometimes a particular scene is replaced; other times the pace is adjusted by shortening one and lengthening another. The goal is to make all editing changes at this stage, since doing so later will significantly add to costs.

Once the rough cut is approved, the spot needs to be finalized. This includes color correction to make sure that all the scenes meld properly, recording the official voice-over, adding the final music, and laying all the tracks over the video footage.

Choosing music can become a sticking point when finalizing a commercial. Direction is often difficult to communicate clearly. Adjectives such as livelier can be difficult to interpret. We once collaborated on a commercial where the music was changed seven times before the client finally agreed to go with the initial agency recommendation.

Sometimes the client falls in love with the scratch track and wants to keep it. However, they can't because another advertiser is already using it. Sadly, no matter how good the final music is, they will always be disappointed.

5. Shipping: one to two weeks

Once the commercial is completed, it is duplicated and shipped overnight to the stations that will be running it. Duplication is generally an overnight process, and is outsourced to specialty companies that invest in high-speed, high-quality equipment.

Different forms of media require different lead times: network programming generally requires one week, syndicated programming two.

AT&T

Now that we have reviewed a normal timeline, here's one from a commercial we produced for AT&T in one week. It was an extraordinary experience, and it would not have been possible without a very experienced creative team, an ultra cooperative client, and no cost restraints.

Of course it helped that the sheer volume of work produced for AT&T—over 30 commercials a year for just this division— meant that the stakes were not as high as they would have been for a typical client. If the spot didn't work, they would simply pull it and put another on in its place. But, it was actually quite successful, and virtually indistinguishable from its peers when completed.

This is what the timeline looked like:

Monday and Tuesday: Scout locations

This commercial was about real small business owners who used and preferred AT&T. We chose locations in the New York City area, using a variety of different business types to add visual interest, with many located close together so we didn't need to travel as much.

Wednesday: Pre-production meeting

All the location, talent, wardrobe and prop decisions were reviewed and approved.

Thursday and Friday: Shoot

We did two 12-hour days of shooting, mostly in Manhattan, some on City Island, which gave us a nice diversity of backgrounds.

Saturday and Sunday: Post-production

The creatives and editors spent the entire weekend in a dark room to complete the edit. Since we had to open the editing facility especially for this job, overtime charges were involved.

We also had to obtain client approvals on Sunday night, so we sent the tapes via car service to the houses of those who needed to approve it. If they had not made themselves available for approvals, we would not have been able to proceed.

<u>Monday: Tape delivery & airing</u>

I hand delivered these tapes myself, since the networks have their offices in Manhattan. Technically, what we did was not allowed—remember the one-week lead time—but money talks.

Monday night the commercials ran on the network evening news.

On Tuesday, we met with the director and crew again to shoot more footage for the pool-outs: a toll-free-phone-number version, and an international version. The director, who had seen the commercial on the news the previous night, said: "This is the first time I've seen something on-air while I was still shooting it."

24. Conclusion

These days, I look back on my career in advertising with great fondness. It's a fascinating industry with many challenges. The people are terrific, very smart and creative, and for the most part, lots of fun. And, while I have moved on to a new chapter in my life, I still maintain a strong passion for advertising and respect for its practioners.

Now that I'm in academia, I realize how confusing understanding advertising can be, since it isn't really linear. What I have attempted to do for my classes, and now in this book, is to distill the process down to its core essence.

While researchers will continue to unearth new facts about consumers and communication, new media options will evolve, and new creative techniques will emerge, the basics will still apply. They are:

1. Know everything there is to know about your target.

2. Find a consumer insight that will allow you to make an emotional connection with them.

3. Build a targeted, integrated communication plan that includes a "wow" tactic to get their attention.

4. Develop tightly focused creative briefs that speak directly to their needs and wants.

5. Hire collaborators that can bring something to the party and help you maximize your vision.

Afterward

When I began thinking about teaching advertising, I realized that I was lucky if I could remember one thing from each course that I had taken in college. Assuming my students would face a similar situation, I asked myself, what would be the one thing that I would want people to take away from my classes?

While I was pondering the issue, my nephew Steven McGlynn came to visit for a few days with his buddy Brad, to take in some Yankee games and the local bar scene. I immediately turned them into my own private focus group and began quizzing them on their reaction to ads, primarily the ones for beer, which have always baffled me.

When I saw Steven again over the holidays, he told me, "Thanks to you, I will never think about advertising the same way again. Now, every time I see an ad, I ask myself: Is this a good ad? Does it make me want to buy something?"
I thought: bingo.

Because, once you ask yourself that question, you immediately change the paradigm, and open yourself up to thinking in an entirely new direction. Needless to say, that is the ultimate goal for any educator -- to help people see and explore new possibilities. And, if the lesson is applied to other situations beyond advertising, I'll be even more delighted.

Please feel free to check out my blog about current advertising issues at http://pjlehrer.blogspot.com. Interesting comments are always welcome!

Regards,
Prof. Lehrer

Glossary

80/20 rule: Marketing principle formulated by Joseph Juran, which states that in any given category, 20% of the people account for 80% of the sales.

A&U: Attitude & Usage – broad omnibus research study that seeks to determine underlying trends for categories and products.

Ad hoc: Temporary

Art director: The member of the creative development team who is primarily responsible for visuals.

Baby Boomers: People born from 1946 -- 1964. Approximate size: 78 million.

Bleed: When the live area of a 2-D creative piece extends to the outer edges of the page.

Brand: The space a product or service occupies in the consumer's mind.

BrainReserve: Consumer trend company founded by Faith Popcorn.

B-to-B: Business-to-business.

CCO: Chief Creative Officer

CPM: Cost-per-thousand – calculated using the following formula: $CPM = (Cost\ of\ media\ buy / Total\ impressions) \times 1000$. CPMs are used to compare different media properties based on cost efficiency.

Demographics: Population or consumer statistics regarding socioeconomic factors such as age, income, sex, occupation, education, family size and the like.

Differentiator: A specific aspect of a product or service that makes it different from the competition.

Editorial adjacencies: Running an advertisement next to compatible editorial.

Flighting: Scheduling advertising in an off again on again pattern in order to achieve continuity with a limited budget.

Focalyst: Research company specializing in data about the Baby Boomer market (Born 1946 – 1964).

Focus groups: Groups of 6–12 individuals who respond to specific stimuli, and provide open-ended feedback guided by a moderator, whose role is to minimize group think and maximize individual participation.

Frequency: The average number of times that someone in the target market will see campaign communications.

FTC: Federal Trade Commission

Gen X: People born from 1965 -- 1979.
Approximate size: 45 million

Gen Y: People born from 1980 – 1994.
Approximate size: 80 million.

Heavy-up: Concentrating advertising over a specific time period in order to create more impact.

Heavy users: Individuals who are part of the 20% of users who account for 80% of sales (See 80/20 rule).

IMC: Integrated Marketing Communications – using a variety of media types in a coordinated communications effort.

Impressions: The raw number of exposures for a communications effort. Since the number includes multiple exposures, it does not accurately portray the number of individuals exposed.

Intelliquest: Resource for category and product demographic information for the technology and telecom industries.

IPO: Initial Public Offering.

LNA: Leading National Advertisers – resource for advertising spending data.

Minimum communication thresholds: The amount of repetitions necessary to create awareness, understanding and persuasion.

MRI: Mediamark Research & Intelligence – one of two primary resources for category and product demographic information (see Simmons).

Niche target: A small well-defined segment with strong commonalities that make them more likely to purchase a product or service.

Nielsen: Resource for information about television audience size and composition.

Positioning statement: A standard format used to express strategy.

To _____*(target market)*_____,who _____*(consumer insight)*_____, Brand XYZ _____*(frame of reference)*_____, is _____*(point of difference)*_____, because _____*(reasons to believe)*_____.

Primary research: Research that is generated by a specific company.

Product placement: Integration of product promotion into content.

Psychographics: Criteria for segmenting consumers by lifestyle, attitudes, beliefs, values, personality, buying motives, and/or extent of product usage.

Qualitative research: Research that allows subjects to provide open-ended answers; typically takes the form of focus groups.

Quantitative research: Research that is formatted so that responses can be tallied and evaluated. Statistically significant populations are used so that data may be accurately projected nationally.

Reach: The percentage of the target market that will see the campaign.

Recency theory: Running a low level of communications consistently throughout the year to constantly remind the consumer of a product or service's existence. Most frequently used for well established brands with flat seasonality.

ROI: Return on investment.

Roll-out: Advertising a product or service in a limited geographical region, and then gradually adding new markets over time. Generally used when manufacturing capabilities limit the ability to launch a product nationally.

Rule of Threes: Consumers need to be exposed to an idea three times before they remember it.

Secondary research: Research that is done by a third party.

Silent Generation: People born from 1922 – 1945. Approximate size: 50 million.

Simmons: One of two primary resources for category and product demographic information (see MRI).

Spot media: Media placed in individual markets.

SRDS: Resource for information about magazine publication schedules and advertising rates.

Statistically significant: Data from a sample size that is large enough to be projected nationally with accuracy.

Storyboard: Visual representation of broadcast creative which includes key visuals and complete copy.

Substantiation: Research used to support an advertising claim.

Syndication: Television shows that run nationally on different networks locally, often at different times as well. Examples include: *Oprah* and *Jeopardy*.

Target market: A group of people that a piece of communications is designed to reach.

Target segment: A specific portion of a target market that shares commonalities.

TNS: Resource for advertising spending data.

Triple-bid: Asking three vendors to provide specs and costs for a job, so that approaches and prices can be compared.

Turn-key: A complete package that provides all the elements necessary for the project so that it can be implemented with little additional effort on the part of the purchaser.

VALS: A psychographic classification system developed by SRI Consulting Business Intelligence used to classify consumers based on primary motivation and resources.

VNR (Video News Release): Marketer generated communications, designed to appear as content, and integrated into news programming without attribution.

Wear-out: When a piece of communications has run so frequently that is it no longer effective.

"Wow" tactic: A specific communications tactic that will allow the campaign to breakthrough clutter, and capture the interest of the target market.

Yankelovich: Resource for data about consumer behavior trends.

Notes & References

Chapter 1
[1] Arens, W.F., Weigold, M.F. & Arens, C. (2009). *Contemporary Advertising*. New York: McGraw-Hill Irwin, p. 139-140.

[2] Elliott, S. (2007). American Express Gets Specific and Asks, 'Are you a cardmember?'. nytimes.com. Retrieved April 6, 2007, from http://www.nytimes.com/2007/04/06/business/media/06adco.html?ei=5090

[3] Jared Fogle. (2009). *NNDB*. Retrieved January 20, 2009, from http://www.nndb.com/people/955/000044823/

[4] York, E. (2008). Subway Can't Stop Jonesing for Jared. Adage.com. Retrived February 20, 2008, from http://adage.com/print?article_id=125142

Chapter 2
[1] Barovick, H., Cruz, G., Salemme, C., Sharples, T., Silver, A., & Stinchfield, K. (2008, March 17) Milestones. *Time*.

[2] Pregnancy Symptoms & Solutions. (2009) w*hattoexpect.com*. Retrived January 21, 2009, from http://www.whattoexpect.com/pregnancy/symptoms-and-solutions/hemorrhoids.aspx

[3] Kerka, S. (1993) Women and Entrepreneurship. *ERIC Digest.org*. Retrieved April 12, 2009, from http://www.ericdigests.org/1994/women.htm

[4] Drinking Juice Slashes Alzheimer's (2006) *Fisher Center for Alzheimer's Research Foundation*. Retrieved September 15, 2006, from http://www.alzinfo.org/newsarticle/templates/newstemplate.asp?articleid=3&zoneid=1

Chapter 3
[1] Gray, J. (1992). *Men are from Mars, Women are from Venus*. New York: Harper Collins

[2] Dictionary of marketing terms. (2009). *allbusiness.com*. Retrieved January 20, 2009, from
http://www.allbusiness.com/glossaries/demographics/4963084-1.html

[3] Dictionary of marketing terms. (2009). *allbusiness.com*. Retrieved January 20, 2009, from
http://www.allbusiness.com/glossaries/psychographics/4956688-1.html

[4] Vranica, S. (2006). Yo! Smirnoff Raps for Malt Beverage. *The Wall Street Journal.* August 10, 2006, p.B3.

Chapter 4
[1] Shiv, B.& Fedorikhin, A. (1999, December). Heart and Mind in Conflict: The Interplay of Affect and Cognition in Consumer Decision Making. *Journal of Consumer Research*, 278-292

[2] Neff, J. (2007, September 24). Soft Soap. *Advertising Age*.

[3] Jeffers, M. (2005, September 12) Behind Dove's 'Real Beauty'. *Adweek*. p. 34-35.

[4] Vranica, S. (2008, April 10) Can Dove Promote a Cause and Sell Soap? *The Wall Street Journal.* p. B6

Chapter 5
[1] Levere, J. (2007). Scrambling to Get Hold of a Passport. *nytimes.com* Retrived January 21, 2009, from
http://www.nytimes.com/2007/01/23/business/23passport.html

Chapter 6
Guinness recommendation © PJ Lehrer 2009

Chapter 7
[1] Neff, J. (2009). Guess which medium is as effective as ever: TV. *adage.com*. Retrived February 23, 2009, from
http://adage.com/print?article_id=134790

[2] (2009, August 28). 114.9 Million U.S. Television Homes Estimated for 2009-2010 Season. *Blog.nielsen.com*. Retrieved July 9, 2010, from

http://blog.nielsen.com/nielsenwire/media_entertainment/1149-million-us-television-homes-estimated-for-2009-2010-season/

3 (2010, May 27). "American Idol" finale lowest audience since 2002. *In.reuters.com*. Retrieved July 9, 2010 from http://in.reuters.com/article/idINTRE64Q50L20100527

4 Steinberg, B. (2009, October 26). 'Sunday Night Football' Remains Costliest TV Show. *Adage.com*. Retrieved July 9, 2010, from http://adage.com/article?article_id=139923

5 Vranica, S. (2006, May 8). Where the ad dollars go. *The Wall Street Journal*. pR4.

Chapter 8
1 Loechner, J. (2009, November 9). Radio Dominant Audio Device. *Mediapost.com*. Retrieved November 11, 2009, from http://www.mediapost.com/publications/index.cfm?fa=Articles.showArticle&art_aid=117009

2 (2006, October 23). Radio Listeners Stay Tuned During Commercials. *Adweek* p1

Chapter 9
1 Kelly, K. (2009, 2008, November 23). Becoming Screen Literate. *The New York Times*. Retrieved March 13, 2009, from http://www.nytimes.com/2008/11/23/magazine/23wwln-future-t.html?_r=1&ref=magazine

2 Ives, N. (2007, May 22). Young Adults Bigger Mag Readers Than Their Parents. *adage.com*. Retrived May 24, 2007, from: http://adage.com/print?article_id=116831

3 Zanville, S., Baron, R., & Ephron, E. (2002). *Advertising Media Planning*. New York: McGraw-Hill Professional, p65

4 Moses, L. (2008, June 16). Best use of print. *AdWeek*. pSR16

5 Moses, L. (2008, February 25). Off The Page. *AdWeek* p14-17
6 Scordo, Lizbeth. (2008, October). Striking Oil. *Relish*. p6

[7] Sass, E. (2009, March 3). MPA: Mag Sites Boost Traffic 11%. *mediapost.com*. Retrived March 13, 2009, from http://www.mediapost.com/publications/index.cfm?fa=Articles.showArticle&art_aid=101406

[8] Moses, L. (2008, June 16). Best use of print. *AdWeek*. pSR16

[9] (2009). Paid circulation: then and now. *adage.com*. Retrieved from, March 13, 2009 from http://adage.com/images/random/0309/4-1990s-030909.pdf

[10] Sass, E. (2009, February 26). Rocky Mountain Bye: 150-Year-Old Denver Daily Dies. *mediapost.com*. Retrieved March 13, 2009, from: http://www.mediapost.com/publications/index.cfm?fa=Articles.showArticle&art_aid=101134

[11] Ives, N. (2009, March 9). Where 1990's Top Papers Are Now. *adage.com*. Retrieved March 9, 2009 from http://adage.com/mediaworks/article?article_id=135094

Chapter 10

[1] Sass, E. (2008, August 11). Out-of-Home Not Running Out-of-Gas, Report Finds Outdoor Exposure Stable. *mediapost.com*. Retrieved March 19, 2009, from http://www.mediapost.com/publications/index.cfm?fa=Articles.showArticle&art_aid=88235

[2] (2006, September). Interactive Billboards Land at Chicago. *Other Advertising*, p13

[3] (2006, October). Magic Bus. *Other Advertising*, p12

Chapter 11

[1] Shankland, S. (2009, January 15). Goggle conquers 2008 US search market. *CNET News.com*. Retrieved March 30, 2009, from http://www.zdnetasia.com/news/internet/0,39044908,62050101,00.htm

[2] Vranica, S. (2006, May 8). Running the show – where the ad dollars go. *The Wall Street Journal, Small Business (A special report)*, pR4

3 (2008, September 9). How Circuit City Uses How-To Videos to Boost Customer Loyalty. *marketingsherpa.com*. Retrived September 11,2008, from http://www.marketingsherpa.com/article_print.html?id=30817

4 Casey, N. (2007, December 6). Nike, New Coach Chase Serious Runners. *The Wall Street Journal*, pB7.

5 Lowenstein, K. (2009, October 15). Public Eye. *Time Out New York*, p1.

6 Story, L. (2007, October 14). The New Advertising Outlet: Your Life. *The New York Times*, Sunday Business p1, 11-12.

7 Dodes, R. (2006, April 1-2). The New Web Exclusives. *The Wall Street Journal*, p3.

8 (2008, February 25). Pinning Down One Very Mobile Group. *AdWeek*, p24.

9 (2009, March 23). Mobile Internet, TV and Video Gaining Ground. *mediapost.com*. Retrieved March 23, 2009, from *http://www.mediapost.com/publications/index.cfm?fa=Articles.showArticle&art_aid=102589*

10 Loechner, J. (2008, January 30). Marketers Say eMail Strongest Performing Media Buy. *www.mediapost.com*. Retrieved January 31, 2008, from http://www.mediapost.com/publications/index.cfm?fa=Articles.showArticle&art_aid=75156

11 Loechner, J. (2009, March 27). Relevant Advertising With Bucks Off Captures Online Consumers. *mediapost.com*. Retrieved March 30, 2009, from http://www.mediapost.com/publications/?fa=Articles.showArticle&art_aid=102593

12 High, K., Morrissey, B., Parpis, E. (2007, June 25). The "Evolution" of Advertising. *AdWeek*, p6.

13 Vranica, S. (2007, December 27). Best of Ads, Worst of Ads. *Wall Street Journal*, pB1.

14 Neff, J. (2006, October 29). Better ROI From YouTube Video Than Super Bowl Spot. *adage.com*. Retrieved November 4, 2006, from http://adage.com/print?article_id=112835

[15] Stone, B. (2009, March 29). Is Facebook Growing Up Too Fast? *Wall Street Journal*, p BU1

[16] Harris, J. (2009, December 16). Making Online Social Networks Profitable: Balancing New Advertising Methods with User Satisfaction. *Thesis submitted for Master of Science in Management and Systems at the Division of Programs in Business School of Continuing and Professional Studies New York University*

Chapter 12
[1] Baar, A. (2008). TD Bank is 'At your convenience' through January. *Mediapost.com*. Retrieved December 1, 2008, from http://www.mediapost.com/publications/?fa=Articles.san&s=95483&Nid=49878&p=210194

[2] (2006). What is the oldest ad medium?. *Other Advertising*.

[3] (2008, June 24). Understanding the True Value of Multi-platform Advertising. *IMMI; Integrated Media Measurement Inc.* Retrieved April 12, 2009, from http://www.immi.com/pdfs/2008-06-24_WP_Crossplatform.pdf

[4] Story, L. (2007). Anywhere the Eye Can See, It's Likely to See an Ad. *The New York Times*. Retrieved March 4, 2009, from http://www.nytimes.com/2007/01/15/business/media/15everywhere.html?_r=1&adxnnl

[5] Gorell, R. (2008). How to Elf Yourself out of Millions. *grokdotcom.com*. Retrieved February 12, 2009, from http://www.grokdotcom.com/2008/02/08/elf-yourself-campaign/

[6] "Healthy hearts, healthy soups, healthy sales.", (2008). *mecglobal.com*. Retrieved November 19, 2009, from http://www.mecglobal.com/campbell-s-healthy-request-soups/

[7] Goetzl, D. (2009). DVR Habits Among Upscale Viewers. *Mediapost.com*. Retrieved January 7, 2009, from http://www.mediapost.com/publications/?fa=Articles.printFriendly&art_aid=97840

Chapter 13

[1] Newman, E. (2007). Like Your Dad? Let Dockers Tell Him So. *brandweek.com*. Retrieved June 8, 2007, from http://www.brandweek.com/bw/news/recent_display.jsp?vnu_content_id=1003596511

Examples © PJ Lehrer 2009

Chapter 14

[1] Herbert E. Krugman. (1972) Why Three Exposures May Be Enough. *Journal of Advertising Research* 12, 6 (1972): 11-14

[2] Lashley, K. S. (1951). The problem of serial order in behavior. In Jeffress, L. A., editor, *Cerebral Mechanisms in Behavior*. Wiley, New York.

George A. Miller. (1956) The Magical Number Seven, Plus or Minus Two. *The Psychological Review*, vol. 63, Issue 2, pp. 81-97

Simon, H.A. (1974). How big is a chunk? *Science*, 183, 482-488.

[3] Anders, G. (2007, October 1), Marketers Get Creative to Stave Off Ad Fatigue. *The Wall Street Journal*. pB5.

[4] Feuer, J. (2003), Cannes Inspires P&G Marketing Boss. *Adweek.com*. Retrieved June 20, 2003, from http://www.allbusiness.com/marketing-advertising/4126330-1.html

[5] Three Screen Viewing Reaches New Heights. (2009) *mediapost.com*. Retrieved March 3, 2009, from www.mediapost.com

[6] Bornstein, R.F., Kale, A.R., & Cornell, K.R. (1990) Boredom as a limiting condition on the mere exposure effect. *Journal of Personality & Social Psychology*, 58, 791-800

[7] Ephron, E. (1997, July/August). Recency Planning. *Journal of Advertising Research*, p 61 – 64

[8] US TV Households by Market. (2009), *tvb.org*. Retrieved February 15, 2009, from http://www.tvb.org/rcentral/markettrack/us_hh_by_dma.asp

Chapter 15
MPS Communications plan © PJ Lehrer 2009

Chapter 16
[1] Tybout, A., Calkins, T. (2005). *Kellogg on Branding*. New Jersey: Wiley P:13

[2] Arens, William F., Weigold, Michael F., Arens, Christian (2007). *Contemporary Advertising: Edition 11*. New York: McGraw-Hill Irwin

[3] Ricco, R.B. (2008) The Influence of argument structure on judgements of argument strength, function and adequacy. *The Quarterly Journal of Experimental Psychology*, 61 (4), 641-664

Chapter 17
[1] Frequently Asked Advertising Questions: A Guide for Small Business. *ftc.gov*. Retrieved April 20, 2009, from http://www.ftc.gov/bcp/edu/pubs/business/adv/bus35.shtm

[2] (2008, June 6). Gillette Fusion case study: developing a US$1 billion brand. *market-research-report.com*. Retrieved April 20, 2009 , from http://www.market-research-report.com/datamonitor/CSCM0171.htm

[3] Sellers, T. (2006, December 6). Consumers develop a passion for all things pomegranate. *cfbf.com*. Retrieved December 6, 2006 from http://www.cfbf.com/agalert/AgAlertStory.cfm

[4] Zaslow, J. (2006, March 18-19). Happiness Inc. *Wall Street Journal*, p1, p5.

[5] Mahoney, S. (2007, November 27). Poll: Economy To Stifle The Season's Do-Gooderism. *mediapost.com*. Retrieved November 30, 2009, from http://www.mediapost.com/publications/index.cfm?fa=Articles.showArticle&art_aid=71562&passFuseAction=PublicationsSearch.showSearchResults&art_searched=charitable%20causes%20and%20sales%20&page_number=2

[6] (2007, October 15). Self Study: Women Willing To Pay Premium for a Cause. *AdWeek*, p38.

[7] Baar, A. (2008, March 12). Pedigree Adoption Campaign Drives Dog Food Sales. *mediapost.com*. Retrived, March 16, 2008 from http://www.mediapost.com/publications/index.cfm?fa=Articles.showArticle&art_aid=78294&passFuseAction=PublicationsSearch.showSearchRelts&art_searched=pedigree&page_number=3

[8] (2006). Ford Hybrid sales up +115%. *Ford Truck Enthusiasts*. Retrieved 12/1/08 from: http://www.ford-trucks.com/news/idx/13/293/2006/article/Ford_Hybrid_Sales_Up_115_Percent.html

Pom Juice poster courtesy of Pom Wonderful Inc. © 2002

Chapter 18
[1] Neumeier, M. (2006). *The Brand Gap*. Berkeley: New Riders, p9

[2] Guerrera, F. (2007, May 23). GE doubles 'green' sales in two years. *ft.com* Retrieved, May 15, 2009 from http://www.ft.com/cms/s/0/1f6db26a-0951-11dc-a349-000b5df10621.html

[3] Aaker, David A. (1996). Building Strong Brands. New York: The Free Press, New York, NY, p. 319.

[4] Frampton, J. (2008, October 18). The Red Thread: The True Power of a Well-Managed Brand. *Interbrand.com*. Retrived, June 18, 2009 from http://www.interbrand.com/paper.aspx?paperid=24&langid=1000

[5] Lucent Technologies Case Study © McCann-Erickson 1996

Photos © Edward Lindquist 1989, 2000

Chapter 19
Creative Brief format and examples © PJ Lehrer 2009

Chapter 20
Asphalt Green creative brief © PJ Lehrer 2009

Chapter 22

[1] Payne, J. & Nadel, L. (2004). Sleep, dreams and memory consolidation: The role of the stress hormone cortisol. *Learning & memory.* Retrived June 18, 2009 from http://learnmem.cshlp.org/content/11/6/671.full

[2] (2006, March 26). The Lines Don't Form Here. *The New York Times.* p3.

[3] "The Scout Report" (2006, October 6). In Wisconsin, a state renowned for its cheese, competition arises from the farms and factories of California. *coutwise.edu.* Retrieved December 12, 2009, from *http://scout.wisc.edu/Reports/ScoutReport/2006/scout-061006-inthenews.php*

[4] Fabre-Thorpe, M., Delorme, A., Marlot, C. & Thorpe, S. ((2001, March). A Limit to the Speed of processing in Ultra-Rapid Visual Categorization of Novel Natural Scenes. *Journal of Cognitive Neuroscience.* Vol.13, Issue 2, p 171-180

Chapter 23

Process charts © PJ Lehrer 2009

Index

80/20 rule, 7

A

Absolut, 96
American Airlines, 130
American Express, 4, 19
Anheuser Busch, 98-99
Asphalt Green, 119-122
AT&T, 8-9, 18, 87, 93-95, 105, 128, 130, 153-155

B

Barkinglot, 37
Black & Decker, 84
Bours, Jeroen, 20, 106
Branding, 101-108
        brand equity, 104-105
        global, 105-106

C

California Cheese, 132
Campbell's, 63-64, 92
Chevy, 135
Coca-Cola, 104-106
communications planning, 59, 71-80
        IMC, 59
        MPS, 77-80
        objectives, 65-69, 110-111, 115, 120
        strategies, 65-69
        tactics, 60-62, 65-69
consumer insights, 15-18, 64, 66-70, 77, 98, 113, 116, 118, 121
Country Inn Rice Dishes, 24
CPMs, 73-74
creative brief, 109-122

D

Dell, 103
demographics, 11-12, 14
DeWalt Power Tools, 84
Disney, 16, 114-117
Dockers, 66
Dove, 16, 53, 56

E

executional formats, 127, 135